Walks in Welcoming Places

WALKS IN WELCOMING PLACES

Outings in the Northeast for Strollers of All Ages and the Disabled

MARINA HARRISON AND
LUCY D. ROSENFELD

Drawings by Lucy D. Rosenfeld

MICHAEL KESEND PUBLISHING, LTD
NEW YORK

Acknowledgments

We would particularly like to acknowledge Gillian Rosenfeld for the inspiration for this book. In addition, we would like to thank Bob Samuels, Helen Bruner, Patricia Bartels, Peter Rosenfeld, Andy Boose, Nadège Brossollet, and, as always, our encouraging publisher, Michael Kesend.

First Publication 1995
Published by Michael Kesend Publishing, Ltd.
1025 Fifth Avenue, New York, NY 10028

Harrison, Marina, 1939–
Walks in welcoming places : walks in the northeast for the strollers of all ages and the disabled / Marina Harrison and Lucy D. Rosenfeld : drawings by Lucy D. Rosenfeld.
p. cm.
Includes index.
ISBN 0-935676-49-5
1. Northeastern States—Guidebooks. 2. Walking—Northeastern States—Guidebooks. 3. Handicapped—Travel—Northeastern States—Guidebooks. 4. Aged—Travel—Northeastern States—Guidebooks. I. Rosenfeld, Lucy D., 1939– . II. Title.
F106.H248 1995 95-8792
917.404'43—dc20 CIP

Contents

Preface

As the authors of three previous guidebooks of the northeast, we are happy to be able to meet many of our readers' requests for outings suitable for the strollers of all ages and the disabled. This book includes a compilation of walks to unique artistic, historic, and natural sites.

Our older readers and those with young children are more active than ever before and we hope will welcome our suggestions for intriguing excursions within our region. The sites described are accessible by car and are easy, flat walking once you get there.

Almost all sites are wheelchair or stroller accessible, often with paved walkways, and are so identified at the end of each write-up. Please note: We strongly urge you to telephone each site in advance to make sure that its standards meet your personal requirements. We have also included sensory gardens for the visually impaired. In addition, a number of these outings are highly appropriate for grandparents or parents who have children in tow.

We think you will find this book useful, as well as enjoyable, as you explore these unusual places. We have included a variety of public and botanic gardens, sculpture parks, unspoiled villages, architectural sites, college campuses, artists' homes, shore walks, and both urban and rural delights.

As you travel throughout the northeast, we hope you will take our book along and will have many memorable and pleasant adventures.

Words from Our Readers

If you're disabled, or if the years have stolen the spring from your step, you have a perfect excuse for sitting at home. Getting out is difficult—staying put is oh so comfortable.

Don't yield to the temptation. It's a trap. The more you stay home, the more your world shrivels. The less you go out, the stranger and more threatening it becomes. When you withdraw, your family and friends also pull away from you.

Because I'm a disabled travel writer, people often ask me which country is easiest for people with physical handicaps to tour. The answer is easy. It's the United States. Each year, thanks in part to the Americans with Disabilities Act, it becomes even better.

A dozen years ago, when they discharged me from the Rusk Institute for Rehabilitative Medicine in New York City, getting around was much tougher. I'd lost a nasty bout with Guillain-Barré syndrome, a neurological disorder. As a quadriplegic, I would have to use a wheelchair.

Suddenly, I learned that there weren't many city buses with wheelchair lifts and that few corners had been ramped. Going out was an endless hassle. Most movie houses lacked room for my chair. You'd have to phone ahead to restaurants and ask if you could get in. Forget finding an accessible rest room.

Things are not perfect today but they are much easier now. Every New York City bus has a lift. I'm surprised when I come upon an intersection without curb cuts. All the new movie theaters have spaces for wheelchairs. Restaurant critics routinely include information on accessibility in their reviews. New public buildings are equipped with accessible bathrooms. There's no reason to stay home.

Lucy Rosenfeld and Marina Harrison have filled this book with scenic and interesting places you can comfortably visit. Use it. Your spirits will lift. Your world will expand. You'll have something new to talk about and, most important of all, you'll have a terrific time.

Robert Samuels

Robert Samuels has written about travel for people with disabilities for the past 10 years. These articles, on both US and European destinations, have appeared in many major newspapers and magazines. He also writes regularly on other subjects for a number of publications, including New Mobility, *a prize-winning national magazine for the disabled, where he is Travel Editor.*

WALKS IN WELCOMING PLACES, is right down my alley! I'm 72 years old and have led a vigorous and athletic life including tennis, skiing and backpacking. My husband and I have enjoyed canoeing rivers in the Midwest, rafting on the Colorado, and traveling by barge on a canal in Burgundy.

Many of us older folks are unwilling to be sedentary and want to be adventurous, although our physical abilities are more limited.

Now, expeditions to historic sites have made good outings for us where we can drive close to the spot to be explored. We like gardens—all kinds. But here too, we need to find ones easy to drive to with seats for resting and, if a very large area, paths suitable for a wheelchair. I can still walk some distance, but if visiting a wild life preserve, for instance, need a handy bench on which to take a breather. When near the ocean—we live inland—an excursion to the beach is always exhilarating. I routinely use wheelchairs in museums. It's the only way to go.

This latest in the series of guidebooks by Marina Harrison and Lucy D. Rosenfeld will be a great boon to those of us with limited mobility. We like new experiences but we need to know where we can find these welcoming places.

Helen Bruner

Helen Bruner, who lives on a farm, is a contributor to an arboretum newsletter and has worked in many capacities in politics and the social services.

Walks in Welcoming Places

1

Colonial Park: A Fragrance and Sensory Garden

Somerset County, New Jersey

This extraordinary pair of gardens—one all roses, the other a fragrance and sensory garden—is something special. While it forms only a small one-acre part of a large and spacious county park in Franklin Township, it has a rare quality all its own. Once part of a private estate, the gardens were developed by a horticulturalist when they became part of the public park.

The more unusual of the two gardens is the fragrance and sensory garden. Newly designed with Braille plaques and a low handrail, this garden includes especially interesting flowers and plants to smell and touch. Each example has an unusual quality, such as the soft fuzzy lamb's ears, the fragrant lavender plant, and the tasty mint. As you make your way around the garden, you can feel and smell and even taste these odd, fragrant plants and guess what they are, or read the small plaques. There are soft, spongy plants, prickly plants, and aromatic lemony plants. The flat walkway is made to accommodate those with wheelchairs and the visually impaired, with flagstone paving and intersecting strips of brick to indicate changes in direction. There are many charming

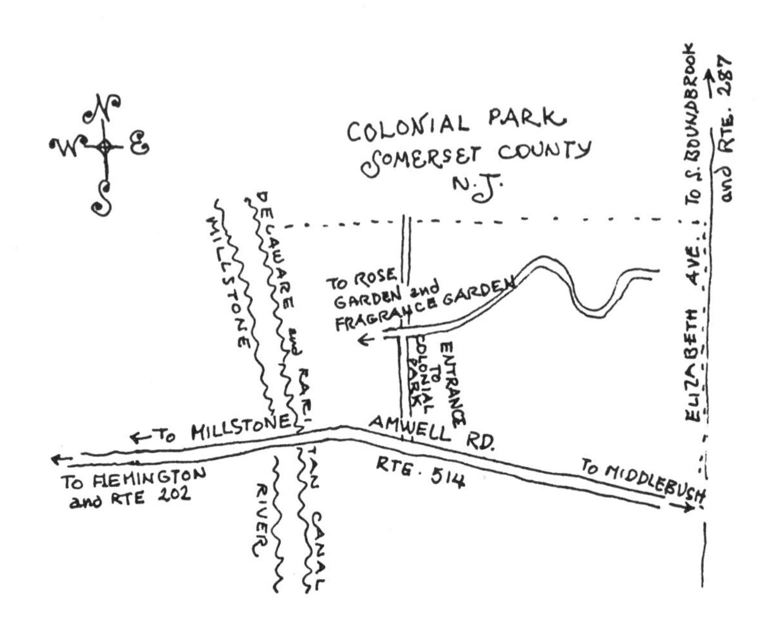

arbored benches for resting. We also recommend this walk for families with children, as it is quite short.

Adjoining the Sensory and Fragrance Garden is the Rose Garden, and what a rose garden it is! Described as "an encyclopedia of roses," the collection includes 4,000 rosebushes (275 varieties) that bloom from early June all the way into fall. One of the sections is called Grandmother's Garden, which contains old hybrid perpetual and hybrid tea roses, some of which date back to the 1820s. Another part has climbing roses, while the Dutch Garden is in the style of a formal rose garden in Holland. It is a beautifully designed garden that is constantly in bloom during the long season. Everything is identified. A walk through it on the flagstone walks can be broken with little rests on arbored benches. For the rose fancier this is a blissful stroll.

If you are of a romantic disposition, you'll find that both gardens have a touch of another time and place about them. We did—on a hot summer day, with the various flowery aromas wafting through the air, and the cool shaded benches inviting us to rest for a moment.

Colonial Park is a vast park, rather overdeveloped, with something for everyone seeking recreation, from paddle boats to a small foresty nature walk, a nice lilac garden, picnic tables, tennis courts, and a playground, in addition to the gardens described above. There are other walks in the park, of course, including a stroll through the arboretum. Guided tours are also available.

INFORMATION

The hours are daily from 10:00 A.M. to 8:00 P.M., from June 1 to November 1. Wheelchair accessible. Telephone: (201) 873-2459.

DIRECTIONS

From the George Washington Bridge take Route 80 west onto Route 287 south. After passing Bound Brook take country route 527 (Easton Ave.). Go right on Cedar Grove Lane. Go right again on Weston Road to Elizabeth Avenue. Entrance to park is on your left on Elizabeth Avenue.

From midtown Manhattan take the Lincoln Tunnel to the New Jersey Turnpike, to Route 287 and follow same directions as above.

2

Snug Harbor: Gardens and Contemporary Art

Staten Island, New York

Snug Harbor on the north shore of Staten Island is a "find" for jaded New Yorkers, art and garden lovers, and anyone else who wants to spend a stretch of time in an unusual and harmonious setting. Originally founded in 1801 as a hospital for retired sailors, its beautiful and expansive grounds and buildings are landmarks. The first of its historic buildings was erected in 1831. There are both large public structures in a variety of architectural styles—ranging from Italianate Revival to Beaux Art—and a row of small Gothic Revival houses once built to accommodate the tradesmen who served the sailors' home. The grounds include the Staten Island Botanical Garden, a conservatory, a concert hall, exhibition space, and much, much more. All these buildings are prettily set on an 80-acre tract of land just across the road from the shoreline and surrounded by outdoor exhibitions of contemporary sculpture. Unlike many such cultural centers, Snug Harbor has an informal air. It is a place that has walkways and byways and open doors; its gardens are invitingly simple and its signs of do's and don'ts minimal. There are no citylike aspects to Snug Harbor; you might be in a place far removed from the bustle and commerce of New York when you wander around here. But Snug Harbor is, indeed, a busy cultural center that includes top attractions (like the Metropolitan Opera and Shakespeare in the Park) in its offerings.

As you enter at the main gate (follow signs on Richmond Road), you will find yourself on a pathway with the parking lot to your left. Walk through the parking lot to the Visitors' Center in one of the main buildings, where you can pick up a map and other material on the Snug Harbor complex of buildings and gardens.

On leaving the visitors' desk, go (directly before you) to Chapel Road to see the wonderful row of five small Victorian cottages. These once housed the baker, gardener, engineer, and farmer who helped to run Snug Harbor in the nineteenth century. Built between 1885 and 1890, they are undergoing renovation with the commendable aim of providing, within the next year or so, living and studio space for resident artists. Several are already occupied. The pathway (Cottage Row) has a duck pond on the left, near which you will see one or two of the outdoor sculptures mentioned in the walk.

Opposite the cottages are the greenhouse and the particularly charming flower gardens. The landscape of the entire park is Victorian in feeling, and so are the garden areas. Among the highpoints of this landscape are the trees, including wonderful willows and a superb collection of flower gardens. The Botanical Garden, which moved to the site in 1975, has put in a variety of small gardens: a formal English perennial garden, a butterfly garden (whose plants are specifically nourishing to butterflies), a Victorian rose garden, an herb garden featuring medicinal and culinary plantings, a "white" garden, which experiments with vertical plantings, a bog garden, and—inside the conservatory—the Neil Vanderbilt Orchid Collection. Any garden enthusiast will enjoy the way these small treasures of planting are arranged—each (in its own season, of course) is a treat. A variety of tours, lectures, and demonstrations are available, but you can also enjoy wandering on your own.

Of particular charm near the gardens is the Chinese-style pagoda built by Charles Locke Eastlake of England. This little pavilion is a concert site and additional Victorian touch to the landscape. At the end of the garden is a dark-green lattice-worked enclosure, which we found particularly appealing. It is planted with charming flowers, and you can sit on the white wrought-iron benches and enjoy a summer's day.

You are now in an area called South Meadow. We suggest turning toward the old dark-red buildings to the east. These house, among other things, the Staten Island Children's Museum, a cheerful place that features all sorts of hands-on exhibitions for the small fry in the family. There are numerous workshops and events with small admission charges.

Near the museum is an old and charming building known as Veterans' Memorial Hall. This is the site of many concerts—from chamber music to jazz. Built in the style of a nineteenth-century parish chapel, the Hall provides an intimate space for small events. In front of the Hall is Chapel Road, once again, and here are the first of the major Greek Revival buildings of the complex. These pale cream, mostly renovated, buildings house a variety of Snug Harbor's organizations: there is the Great Hall, the Music Hall, the Art Lab, and, in the next row, the Main Hall. Art Lab, the art school found at Snug Harbor, also has shows of visual art. Among recent exhibits was an all-island high school show and individual exhibitions in its Atelier Gallery. These grand buildings are both architecturally and historically interesting. In the Main Hall you'll find the Newhouse Gallery, one of Snug Harbor's main attractions. The Newhouse Gallery is Staten Island's principal art space, and as such is an important part of the cultural center. The Gallery also curates the outdoor

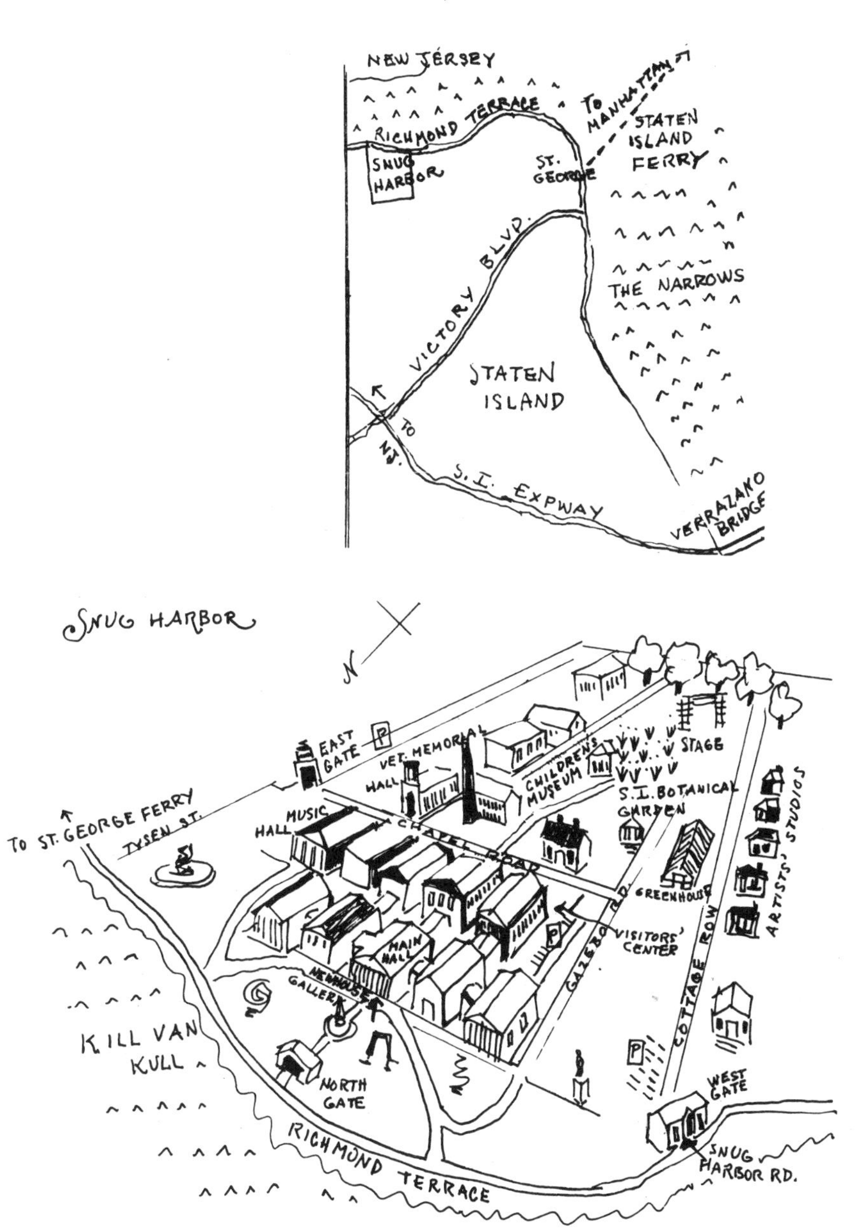
NEW JERSEY
RICHMOND TERRACE
TO MANHATTAN
SNUG HARBOR
ST. GEORGE
STATEN ISLAND FERRY
VICTORY BLVD.
THE NARROWS
STATEN ISLAND
TO N.J.
S.I. EXPWAY
VERRAZANO BRIDGE
SNUG HARBOR
N
EAST GATE
P
VET. MEMORIAL HALL
CHILDRENS MUSEUM
STAGE
S.I. BOTANICAL GARDEN
TO ST. GEORGE FERRY
TYSEN ST.
MUSIC HALL
CHAPEL ROAD
GREENHOUSE
VISITORS' CENTER
ARTISTS' STUDIOS
MAIN HALL
NEWHOUSE GALLERY
GAZEBO RD.
COTTAGE ROW
KILL VAN KULL
NORTH GATE
WEST GATE
RICHMOND TERRACE
SNUG HARBOR RD.

sculpture shows, which are perhaps Snug Harbor's major contribution to New York's contemporary art scene.

Scattered throughout the lovely grounds of the center are about twenty contemporary sculptures at any one time. Sculptures in stone, metal, and mixed media are widely spaced throughout the green fields. (Pick up a guide to the current show at the visitor's center.) The exhibitions are usually mounted around mid-June and run through the month of October, when most of them are taken down. (A few traditional sculptures remain year-round.) The exhibits of contemporary sculpture are very up to date. The installations (which are most interesting to watch—if you happen to visit just before the show begins) include the works of both New Yorkers and others who have sent in slides or have been invited through such arts organizations as DIA in Soho. A tour of all the sculptures will take you about one hour. Among the particularly interesting recent additions was an outdoor play sculpture for children designed by Staten Island sculptor Steve Foust, to be constructed and organized by visiting children. Other recent highpoints included *Memorial to Lost Souls at Sea, 1980* by John Chamberlain, and a steel-skinned "sunken house" by Bill Albertini. A few sculptures are also to be seen indoors in the Great Hall.

INFORMATION

The grounds are open seven days a week (except major holidays), from 8 A.M. to dusk. Open in the evening for occasional special events. Guided tours are offered free, by appointment. We recommend a visit in springtime or early summer, when the fine gardens are at their best.

Mostly wheelchair accessible. Telephone (718) 448-2500 from 9 A.M. to 5 P.M. Monday–Friday.

DIRECTIONS

Snug Harbor is located on the north shore of the island at Richmond Terrace and Snug Harbor Road, conveniently only 2 miles from the Staten Island Ferry Terminal. The Snug Harbor trolley or the S40 bus will get you there. From Manhattan, the best route is by ferry and bus. From Brooklyn, Queens, or Long Island, you should drive via the Verrazano Narrows Bridge (take Bay Street with the harbor on your right, until you find yourself on Richmond Terrace at the ferry terminal. Snug Harbor is on your left, after 2 miles). From New Jersey take the Staten Island Expressway (I-278) to Clove Road/Hyland Boulevard exit. At the traffic light turn left at Clove Road to Richmond Terrace, and right at Snug Harbor.

3

A Walk Through "The Jewel of Long Island Sound"

Southport, Connecticut

This elegant little village, with its scenic harbor on the Sound, is about an hour away from New York City. It is ideal for a leisurely visit, with its pleasant winding roads and salt smell of the sea. You're never more than several blocks from the water. Impeccable 19th-century homes and fine old trees line the streets; its historic district was the first designated in Connecticut. Unlike more bustling waterfront communities such as nearby Fairfield, Southport seems to sit firmly in the 19th century. It has been able to resist commercial expansion and to retain an unusually peaceful flavor.

The Indians sold their claims to Southport in 1661 for "13 coats, two yards apiece, and ye rest in wampum." "Mill River," as it was then called, was at first a prosperous farming area. It began to develop into a village around the time its shipyard was built in 1763. Its natural harbor was small but deep enough to handle ships of up to 100 tons, and it provided surrounding towns with imported luxuries. The local population included wealthy merchants, sea captains, and shipowners. The William Bulkley House at 824 Harbor Road, probably the oldest on the harbor, dates from this period (c. 1760).

However, Mill River's prosperity was temporarily disrupted during the Revolutionary War when the British burned much of the port, leaving only a single building.

In the early decades of the 19th century, Mill River became a more commercial port, home to five schooners, 20 sloops, and one brig. There are still some buildings left from this period. Along Harbor Road you can see several old warehouses that have been converted to residences. In addition, you should note the Gurdon Perry House (c. 1830) at 780 Harbor Road and the Austin Perry House (c. 1830) at 712 Harbor Road.

Soon the town and harbor were growing rapidly and becoming so prosperous that some of the residents even had their own fleets of vessels that sailed to faroff places in the Orient, Europe, or South America. Onion farming was developed in the 19th century and eventually became the town's main source of wealth, bringing the village the nickname "onion capital of America." Southport onions even helped prevent scurvy among the troops during the Civil War.

In the late 19th century the town began to attract New Yorkers looking for a pleasant place to spend the summer. Several fine mansions, as well as the Romanesque-style Pequot Library, date from the Victorian period. Southport became an affluent residential suburb, as new estates were built in the Green Farms and Sasco Hill areas. The Pequot Yacht Club became (and remains) the center of the harbor front. If you enjoy strolling through lanes of graceful old houses with widow's walks amid gentle seaside breezes, you'll like this walk. A history of Southport called "Walking Through History" is available at the Fairfield Historic Society in Fairfield.

Southport is a noncommercial town, not geared for tourists. You are welcome to walk through, but you won't find many restaurants. There are no public beaches or other tourist facilities.

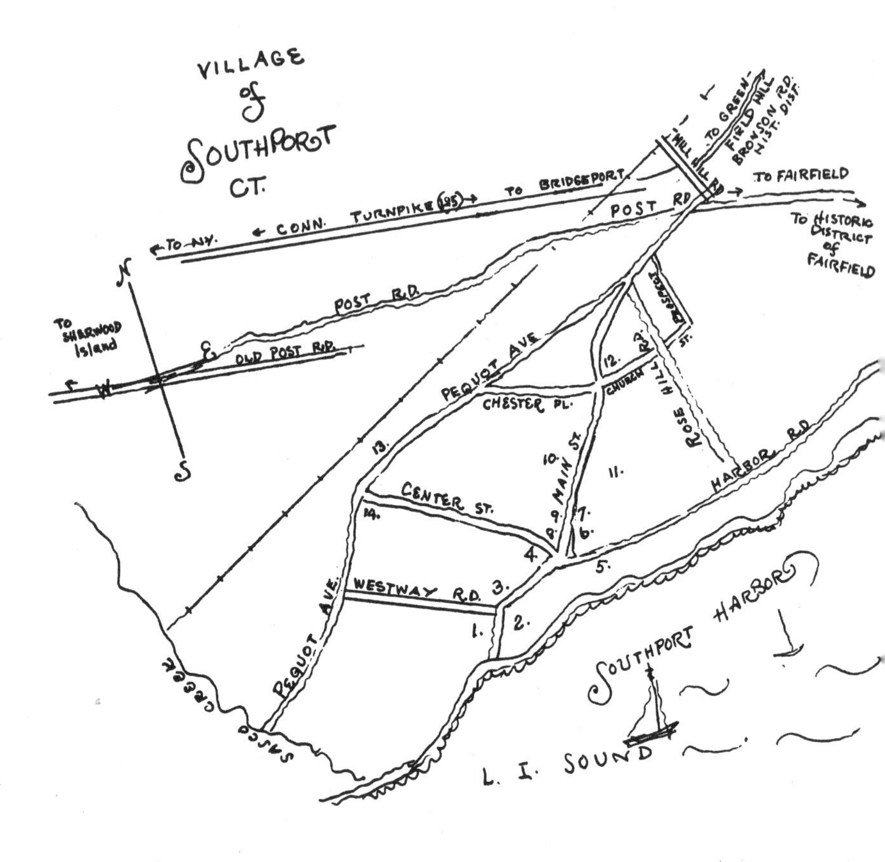

This is an American village walk with its own distinctive flavor. You can easily do this outing in an hour or so, and anyone seeking a real Yankee seaside village walk will enjoy Southport. It's easy on the feet and the energy and relatively simple to reach. Since the boating and swimming facilities are not available to visitors (unless, of course, you arrive by boat), it may be frustrating to small children—even if you promise to go swimming or sailing later.

We recommend that you visit in summer, although spring and fall are lovely too. Special events that might persuade you to go at a particular time include:

Dogwood Festival. This one-week spring festival takes

place in the nearby town of Greenfield Hill (Old Academy and Bronson Roads). The festival is a week-long celebration featuring the 30,000 dogwoods, some of which were originally transplanted after the Revolution. The festival takes place under a tent on the green, features concerts, art shows, sales, and walking tours. Call 203-259-2128 for the exact date and/or luncheon reservations.

Fairfield Day. Celebrated at Jennings Beach on the last Sunday in June, when the town of Fairfield sponsors children's races, egg throwing, musical entertainment, clowns, and even a sky-diving exhibition. No admission charge. Arrive before 11:00 A.M. to avoid traffic and parking problems. Call 203-367-8495 for further information.

In addition to the houses listed below, you should visit the harbor, the focal point of the village. Put your feet in the water! Just viewing Long Island Sound from the coast of Connecticut is a pleasure on a nice day. Southport and some of its surrounding villages have nice waterfronts for watching tides change, boats coming and going, or gulls soaring overhead. Look for seaweed, barnacles, mussels, clams, and other marine life along the sandy coast of the Sound. Gulls and water fowl abound.

For the walk through town, start at the corner of Westway and Harbor roads. (Numbers are keyed to map.)

1. William Bulkley House (c. 1760) at 824 Harbor Road is one of the oldest houses still standing on Southport harbor. It is called a "three-quarters house" meaning that there are four bay windows in the front instead of the more usual five. The house has recently been restored.

2. Old storehouses (early 19th century) at 789 and 825 Harbor Road have been converted to residences. Number 789 was also used as a clubhouse for the Pequot Yacht Club.

3. Gurdon Perry House (c. 1830) at 780 Harbor Road belonged to a wealthy merchant in the early part of the 19th

century. An unpretentious house, it is simpler in style than many later homes built for merchants.

4. Austin Perry House (c. 1830) at 712 Harbor Road is particularly interesting for its portico, which is considered one of the finest of its kind, probably dating from the 1840s.

5. Pequot Yacht Club (c. 1835) at 669 Harbor Road was a warehouse during the port's commercial peak.

6. Jennings Store Building (c. 1834 and later) at 668–70 Harbor Road included the town's first general store and post office. Sections were added during the Victorian period, when the second floor was used as a reading room before the Pequot Library was built.

7. Southport National Bank (1833) at 227 Main Street is now a private residence. Note its Greek Revival style.

8. Hall block and chronicle buildings (1894) at 244 and 252 Main Street were once tenements that housed stores and offices. They were converted into apartments in the 1950s.

9. Southport Savings Bank (1865) at 226 Main Street was built to resemble the roof pitch of the Episcopal Church.

10. Oliver Bulkley House (1859) at 176 Main Street is a wonderful example of early Gothic architecture. For some years this house was called the Pequot Inn; it was used by summer boarders in the 1920s until it was converted into a private home. Note its lovely grounds.

11. Charles M. Gilman House (1873) at 139 Main Street is an interesting combination of Italianate and Gothic styles.

12. Old Academy (1827) at 95 Main Street has served in many capacities. First a private school, it then held church services and finally became a private home in the late 19th century.

13. Pequot Library (c. 1894), located at the intersection of Westway and Pequot Avenue, was designed by a student of H. H. Richardson in Romanesque style and donated to the village.

14. Trinity Episcopal Church (1862), on the corner of Pequot Avenue and Center Street, was built in the Carpenter Gothic style after its original structure (virtually identical) was destroyed by a tornado. The church has a lovely slender spire that can be seen for miles.

INFORMATION

This town is flat and has nice sidewalks appropriate for wheelchairs.

DIRECTIONS

From the west side of Manhattan: West Side Highway, to Cross Bronx Expressway, to Route 95, to exit 19. Follow signs to Southport.

From the east side of Manhattan: FDR Drive to the Major Deegan which becomes Route 95, and follow same directions as above.

4

De Cordova Sculpture Garden: Modern Forms upon a Hill

Lincoln, Massachusetts

The combination of fine modern and contemporary art in an unusually beautiful setting makes the De Cordova Museum and Sculpture Park a remarkable site not to be missed. Situated on the shores of a quiet pond in Lincoln, outside of Boston, its bucolic ambience would be reason enough for a visit: The thirty-five acres of rolling hills, woods, and sweeping lawns with views of the New Hampshire hills, create an inviting environment for a walk. De Cordova also happens to be New England's most important outdoor exhibition space with more than thirty large-scale sculptures on view.

Once the country estate of Julian De Cordova (1851–1945), an eccentric, art-collecting Boston entrepreneur, the property with its odd castlelike structure was bequeathed in 1930 to the town of Lincoln. It was first simply a recreational area; it gradually evolved into a museum, when its potential as an exhibition site was realized. The De Cordova began acquiring and displaying large sculptures by prominent American artists. Since the mid-1980s the museum has included a permanent sculpture park—the only one of its kind in New England—an indoor museum (housed in what once was De Cordova's mansion), and several additional buildings used for classes, studios, and workshops.

Scattered about the spacious grounds—like silent abstract sheep in a pastoral tableau—are modern and contemporary works by a wide variety of American artists. (A map of the grounds and art works is available at the museum desk.) These range from sculptures of such major artists as Alexander Liberman, George Rickey, and Mark di Suvero, to the latest, most innovative environmental pieces. While some works remain at De Cordova as part of their permanent collection (see below), others come and go with the continuous flow of changing exhibits. The sculptures have been carefully placed so they interact harmoniously with the beautifully arranged park, creating a landscape that is in itself a sculpted environment.

Although sculptors of national and international stature are well represented here, a large number of artists shown are from New England. De Cordova is considered to be the premier showcase of the region's most promising artists and is committed to generating public appreciation of its local artistic community. Some of the art has a particular New England focus.

Recently a site-specific work by Gail Rothschild called *Women of the 19th Century: A Conversation* was installed in a quiet hemlock grove. Drawn from the writing of a nineteenth century New England feminist, Margaret Fuller, a transcendentalist colleague of Thoreau and Emerson, it features five giant rocking chairs, each with inscriptions from Fuller and her contemporaries. Placed in each rocking chair is a larger-than-life female figure made of hay held together by chicken wire. The women are kneeling in a way suggestive of the stocks that were used in this region during colonial times. You might draw your own conclusions from this unusual grouping, but the New England context is unmistakable.

Every year De Cordova commissions site-specific works that often speak of environmental issues. A recent show of such work included a sculpture called *Bat House* by Christopher Sproat. It was built as a real haven for these much maligned creatures. Placed in an open field, the sculpture heralds our need to protect these flying mammals. The appropriately Gothic-looking spear-shaped work has a pointed roof and soars fourteen feet into the air. It is without question the only artist-designed bat house you will ever see.

Another unusual installation is Allan Wexler's *Floor Becoming Table on a Hill,* which he located at a leafy site overlooking Flint's Pond. The artist is known for his original—and somewhat eccentric—constructions and arrangements of furniture that reflect the relationships among individuals, architecture, and landscape. This conceptual picnic site includes two sixty-foot-long wooden paths that intersect at a junction where people, landscape, art, architecture, and furniture meet and connect. Philosophy and art aside, you can imagine its being a fine place to dine alfresco.

Another artist, Patrick Dougherty, decided to create something that would respond to the castlelike appearance of the museum's building. The result is *Spin-Offs,* an installation in which natural materials have been woven into conical windswept forms that actually appear to move from the top of the turreted structure to the ground.

These sentiments and concerns for the environment find expression throughout the sculpture park. You may not find all of the specific works mentioned here, since many are not permanently installed. However, the De Cordova has a number of sculptures on its grounds that were gifts to the collection, and that should be on view at all times. Look for:

George Rickey's *Three Lines,* a stainless steel work that focuses on linear movement.

Richard Fishman's *Colleoni,* a contemporary bronze homage to Andrea del Verrochio's equestrian monuments.

Hugh Townley's intriguing concrete work called *Group of Three,* which spells the word ART in abstract manner.

Alexander Liberman's *Cardinal Points,* one of the well-known sculptor's abstract welded steel constructions.

Ed Shay's *Acadian Gyro,* an intriguing bronze construction that he describes as "a skeletal structure of a fish-boat with winged oars" that functions as a symbolic spiritual gyro.

George Greenamyer's *Mass Art Vehicle,* a welded steel construction of a pyramid-shaped vehicle on tracks.

Mags Harries' topiary garden constructions that can be seen as "intimate rooms" when viewed from above.

Lila Katzen's weathered steel *X Notion Like an H,* which explores the "identity" of the letter X.

Paul Matisse's *The Musical Fence,* made of aluminum sounding bars and concrete, a kind of sculptural vibraphone that stretches to more than twenty feet across the lawn.

The museum's gallery shows sometimes relate to the works in the park. A recent museum show featured thirty plastic models created by Allan Wexler in his investigation of ideas for his picnic area.

The De Cordova is an active, vibrant museum complex with many facilities and activities, including classes and workshops. Visits to artists' studios are also arranged. Docent tours of the museum and sculpture park are available for those who enjoy discussing art with others as they view the pieces. However, you are welcome to walk around on your own.

INFORMATION

Museum hours: Tuesday–Friday, 10:00 A.M.-5:00 P.M.; weekends, noon–5:00 P.M.

Sculpture park: open every day of the year from dawn to dusk. There is an inexpensive admission charge for galleries, but not for the sculpture park. Mostly wheelchair accessible, although quite hilly.

Telephone: (617) 259-8355.

DIRECTIONS

De Cordova Museum and Sculpture Park is located on Sandy Pond Road in Lincoln, MA. To get there from Boston: From Route 128: Take exit 28B, Trapelo Road/Lincoln. Take Trapelo Road about 2 1/2 miles to intersection with Sandy Pond Road and follow the signs to De Cordova.

From Mass Pike: Take 128 North and follow directions above.

From Route 93: Take 128 South and follow directions above.

5

Princeton University: Masterworks on Campus

Princeton, New Jersey

American college campuses are well-known for charming shaded walks and Gothic buildings. Few, however, can compare with Princeton University's beautiful campus, nor—of particular interest for us—with its outdoor sculpture collection. Princeton has acquired over the last decades an unusually fine selection of contemporary sculpture. These works are scattered across the campus, making an expedition to see them a most attractive, and artistically satisfying, artwalk.

As you will discover if you set off from the center of the campus, these works have been placed with great care among the walkways and lawns of the campus. You'll see the jagged forms of a Lipchitz against a background of buildings, a huge Picasso in front of Princeton's fine art museum, the gently moving kinetic forms by George Rickey on an open lawn, and works by David Smith, Louise Nevelson, and Isamu Noguchi, among many others. In all, some twenty-one sculptures are to be found on campus, aside from the major collection in the art museum (also open to the public).

If you enjoy strolling on a campus and looking at sculpture as you walk (along with the endlessly fascinating scenes of college life that go on around you), this tour will definitely be a favorite, to which you will return many times. (We recommend a thorough visit to the art museum in conjunction with your walk, for this museum has an outstanding collection of antiquities, European and American paintings, African sculpture, and many other treasures. It is used by scholars from the University and around the world.) Following, however, is specifically a sculpture walk.

Enter the University campus from Nassau Street at the gate opposite Palmer Square. You must go on foot. Park at a meter in town, or leave your car at the University parking lot and take the shuttle bus to campus. The guard at the gate will direct you to the lot or to town parking. Pick up a campus map at the information desk near the gate before you start. (Numbers in this walk refer to this map.)

A fitting beginning to this tour of twentieth century sculpture is a Henry Moore called *Oval with Points.* This commissioned work was installed in 1971 between Stanhope Hall and West College, at F2 on the map. It is made of bronze, its inside surface now burnished from contact with the thousands of students who have lounged on it (to the sculptor's delight). The sculpture bears some resemblance to an elephant skull which was given by Sir Julian Huxley to Moore and placed in the sculptor's garden. "Henry," wrote Huxley, "not only took it to his heart but proceeded to explore its massive outline, its tunnels and cavities, its recesses and blind eye-sockets . . ." You will find the Moore easily recognizable, with or without the knowledge of its relationship to the elephant skull, and you'll enjoy its graceful placement on the green.

An entirely different sculptural experience awaits you at your next stop. Walk on away from the gate to the pathway behind West College. Turn left on the path. At F3 on the map you'll see the slightly undulating forms of George Rickey's

Two Planes, Vertical Horizon II. Don't miss the Rickey work; it is just off the pathway, and somewhat above your head, where its kinetic parts catch the breeze and move almost imperceptibly. Back away to look at it. Rickey is perhaps the leading exponent of this type of sculpture today, though it was Alexander Calder, whose work you will shortly see, who led the way in inventing kinetic sculpture.

Continue on the path and then turn left at its end. Between the University Chapel and Firestone Library (at G2) you'll see the Jacques Lipchitz sculpture called *Song of the Vowels,* one of a series in which the artist worked with a harp motif. This soaring bronze is a cubist structure suggesting a harpist in Lipchitz's familiar curvilinear style. The artist said that the title had to do with a legendary prayer of ancient Egypt in which the forces of nature were called upon. It was installed on the campus in 1969.

In the lobby of Firestone Library itself is another work by a master of contemporary sculpture, Isamu Noguchi. *White Sun* is one in a series of works in various media portraying the sun that the sculptor created in the 1960s. Made of white marble, it is a large, irregular circle with an open center, like many Noguchi sculptures that explore circular and disc-shaped forms.

When you leave the lobby to go back outdoors you'll see another modern "classic" between the Library building and Nassau Street bordering the campus (also G2). This is *Atmosphere and Environment X* by Louise Nevelson (Figure 28), whose work will probably be recognizable to you from many of the other sculpture walks in this book.

Nevelson, a major figure in contemporary sculpture for decades, described her works in her own way:

> Say an architect builds a house. Well, now let's say that he builds the whole thing inside, all the rooms and everything,

but he doesn't have an outside wall. Well, it's not a house, it's a veranda. I want the total house, I don't want my sculpture to be a veranda.

Like other Nevelsons, this one is made of Cor-Ten steel and is quite large—twenty-one feet high and sixteen feet long. It is made up of interlocking black, white and gold geometric shapes set in a shallow relieflike form. You will enjoy watching the play of light and shadow on it if you happen to have a sunny day for your walk, but at any time it is an impressive and monumental work. It was Nevelson's first major work in Cor-Ten steel, a medium that was to become a hallmark of Nevelson sculpture.

Between Firestone and Dickinson Hall (still G2), you'll discover George Segal's memorial to the Kent State massacre: *Abraham and Isaac, in Memory of May 4, 1970, Kent State University.* Segal's very realistic style is a clear contrast with the abstract sculptures we have just seen; his human figures look strikingly real, and though they represent Biblical figures, their contemporary message is very clear.

Walk along Washington Road toward the School of Architecture (G3). If you wish to go inside the building, you'll find in the stairwell Eduardo Paolozzi's imaginative *Marok, Marok, Miosa,* a contemporary work. Paolozzi was the principal exponent of England's junk sculpture movement, making works from found objects.

Here you might gauge your energy and decide whether to cross Washington Road and head several blocks across the campus to the Engineering Quadrangle where three more sculptures are situated. If you want to make this detour, you will walk along Prospect Avenue to Olden Street, where you will turn left and continue until you reach the Engineering School (J2).

At the entrance to the quadrangle you'll see Clement Meadmore's *Upstart 2,* a work made in 1970. This minimalist form, also made of Cor-Ten steel, could be said to resemble a letter of the alphabet or a hard-edge snake; it rises from a slab base, giving an impression of surprising lightness. Meadmore is said to see his sculpture "as being like a person who inhabits a place."

While in the Engineering Quad you can see two more works: Masayuki Nagare's *Stone Riddle* (K2), a contemporary example by the well-known Japanese artist, and *Spheric Theme* by Naum Gabo (K2), a leading figure in Russia's early modern style of constructivism. Gabo's work, a kind of spatial puzzle, involved replacing several of the planes of a cube with interlocking diagonals. The completed stainless steel work, which is eight feet high, is an attempt by Gabo to show that "the visual character of space is not angular . . . I enclose the space in one curved continuous surface."

Turn toward the center of the campus now, walking back along Washington Road toward the gym complex. You will cross Prospect Avenue and Ivy Lane (whether you are coming from the Architecture School or Engineering Quad).

Just beyond Ivy Lane you'll find your next piece of sculpture within the Fine Hall Library, the well-known portrait head of Albert Einstein by the renowned American/British sculptor Jacob Epstein (H5). As you no doubt know, Einstein was a beloved figure in Princeton for many years, and this tribute to him is appropriately placed in the physics library. Epstein's portrait heads were modeled in clay for casting in bronze and are characterized (as this one is) by many small jagged planes that break up the surface of the work.

In the plaza between Fine Hall and Jadwin Hall (H5) is another major work of the Princeton collection: Alexander Calder's *Five Disks: One Empty*. Though this giant work is a stabile rather than one of Calder's more familiar mobiles, it nonetheless has the unmistakable Calder style, with its cutouts and circular and pointed forms of black steel and its mood of playfulness. Though originally painted orange (to honor Princeton's traditional colors) the artist blackened the forms after the work was set on the campus in 1971.

Just behind Fine Hall is Jadwin Hall. Here in the courtyard of the hall (H5) is Antoine Pevsner's *Construction in the Third and Fourth Dimension*. Pevsner was the elder brother of Naum Gabo; together they were active in the constructivist movement in Russia in the 1920s. Pevsner's work is also involved with spatial ambiguity. This sculpture, which rises to more than ten feet, is a bronze abstraction set on a black granite pedestal. It explores the contortion of flat metal planes into shapes that suggest the possibility of infinite continuity.

Cross Washington Road once again and head toward the Computer Science Building, if you are still feeling energetic. (We don't deny that this is a long walk.) Here (F6) you will see Michael David Hall's work *Mastodon VI,* another contemporary sculpture.

Slightly closer is *Sphere VI* by Arnaldo Pomodoro, an Italian sculptor. You'll find this work in Butler College Courtyard (F5). Pomodoro specialized in negative/positive casting, in which parts of the surface were gouged out, giving his forms an imagery of motion from within. *Sphere VI* is a giant polished bronze with a type of interrupted surface that the artist described as "an expression of interior movement."

If you cross the tennis court area to your left, you'll find yourself at some newer dormitory buildings near the train station. Here (E5) is one of the campus' favorite pieces: David Smith's *Cubi XIII.* Situated on the lawn of Spelman Hall, Smith's stainless steel, nine foot high sculpture is one of a series of twenty-eight works that he called *Cubi.* An exploration of Cubist principles in welded steel, these works were designed for outdoor positioning with particular reference to the architecture around them.

Turning back to the heart of the campus, you will pass Dillon Gym and come to a street called Elm Drive. Turn left until you reach a dorm quad called Cuyler. Cross in front of Cuyler to see Prospect Gardens, the lovely formal gardens of the college (and a good place for a quick rest). Prospect House, which overlooks the gardens, has a sculpture on its lawn. It is by the American artist Tony Smith and is called *Moses* (G3).

A strong cubistic work, *Moses* is a painted steel abstraction of angular planes. The artist felt that the parallel uprights suggested the horns of Michelangelo's *Moses* (Moses wears horns because of a misunderstanding by Latinists of the Hebrew for "shining," also the root of the word for horns) and Smith continued the symbolism. But whether or not you see this geometric work as Moses, you will find it interesting to compare with the other studies in contemporary, angular, hard-edged abstractions on this walk.

You arrive next at the Art Museum itself. (We expect you will want to return to it after your last few stops.) You can easily identify it by the imposing Picasso in front of it. *Head of a Woman* (F3) is one of those works that is so identified in our minds with Picasso that it hardly needs introduction. It is constructed of cast concrete, was executed by Carl Nesjar (who did many of Picasso's sculptures) from a maquette made originally in 1962, and was made specifically for this Princeton site. As it was constructed on campus, students watched the process—a unique experience!

Your final stop on the central campus is in the courtyard of Hamilton Hall (E2), back near the gate you originally entered. Here is *The Bride* by British sculptor Reg Butler. This tall slender figure (it stands seven feet high) is a bronze semi-abstract female, whose forms suggest something of the shapes of trees and leaves. The work is in the tradition of British postwar figurative style.

As you leave the campus (don't forget your parking meter!), you may wish to drive to the last two destinations on our sculpture walk. They are both at the Graduate College, which is beyond the golf course to the left of the gate. (See map.) You are headed to A6 where you will want to see Gaston Lachaise's *Floating Figure,* made in 1927. (You may recognize this work from the Museum of Modern Art's Sculpture Garden, where another copy of it is a favorite of sculpture lovers.) A typical example of Lachaise's bronzes, the seated figure balances its rounded forms gently and weightlessly.

Our final destination is to see Kenneth Snelson's *Northwood II* (B6), also in the Graduate College. This is a fitting conclusion to our sculpture walk, for Snelson has become a leading member of the current sculpture stylists. His towering aluminum and steel constructions are supported by cables within the framework. "My concern," he says, "is with nature in its fundamental aspect; the patterns of physical forces in space."

INFORMATION

The University campus is open year-round. This campus is flat and entirely wheelchair accessible. For tours and information telephone (609) 258-3603.

DIRECTIONS

Take the New Jersey Turnpike to exit 9. Take Route 1 south, then Route 571 west to Princeton. Follow signs for the University.

6

Old Westbury Gardens: Elegance on Long Island

Old Westbury, Long Island, New York

The magnificent black iron gates and the grand allée beyond introduce you immediately to the glamorous ambience of Old Westbury Gardens. Here is the splendor of the magnificent European-style formal gardens of the past, their harmonious elegance graced with outdoor sculpture. This is a great estate on the grand scale, bringing to mind hazy romantic scenes involving Edwardian images and moonlit nights. In fact, the gardens are used frequently for movie sets and picture-book weddings, as well as by historians of landscape architecture of the past.

Just a stone's throw from the ultimate contemporary highway landscape, this site is all the more intriguing in its contrast with Long Island sprawl. The estate, built in 1906 by John S. Phipps, a financier and sportsman, is not the only grand house in Old Westbury, where many of the rich and fashionable built their homes at the turn of the century. (Nearby are the William C. Whitney Racing Stables, for example.)

Mr. Phipps hired the London architect George Crawley to construct a Stuart-style "country" mansion, to please his English wife. Westbury House was built atop a hill; its symmetrical elegance is set off by a master plan of landscape design. In fact, the estate is a rare example of landscape and architectural planning that went hand in hand; the complementary designs of the house and its surroundings are worth noting and are of great interest to modern designers.

The interior of the house is elegant and formal. It is open to the public and will appeal to those who enjoy seeing how such country retreats were designed and furnished—from fluted Corinthian columns and French windows, to polished antique tables and Ormolu clocks. You will also find paintings by John Singer Sargent, George Morland, Joshua Reynolds, and Sir Henry Raeburn.

But of particular interest and delight to us were the gardens, which—even without the many sculptures—are a work of art in themselves. Designed by both Crawley and a French landscape architect named Jacques Greber, the master plan called for a formal geometric arrangement of grand allées, softened by English "romantic" or picturesque gardens. The combination, based clearly on the layouts of the grounds of English stately homes, is an unqualified success.

Among its charms are a lake walk—yes, of course, there is a lake—leading to a "Temple of Love," a boxwood garden, a garden with flowers of all the colors of the rainbow, a "ghost walk" of dark hemlock trees, and a walled garden where you can easily imagine—or enjoy—the most romantic of trysts. There are numerous rare and magnificent trees and plantings, including many from the Orient. Almost three hundred species of trees are flourishing at Old Westbury Gardens. Depending on the timing of your visit, you may see profusions of rhododendrons, lilacs, roses, and too many other of nature's most beautiful flowers to list here.

Sprinkled liberally throughout these enchanting areas are neoclassical sculptures and columns and various other art works that add to the ambience of European elegance. Ceres is sheltered in a pergola of wisteria, while a terra-cotta Diana the huntress graces a curving colonnade within the boxwood garden. There are ornamental cherub fountains in pools of lotus and lilies; a pair of bronze peacock statues with topiary tails; an elaborate shell mosaic in the style of Italian grotto decoration of the seventeenth century; a sundial topped with rampant lions; groups of nymphs and satyrs on the roofline of the house; a pair of lead eagles and stone vases on pediments, surrounded by lilacs; and a sculpture of the quasi-mythical athlete, Milo of Cortona, wresting a tree stump from the earth. (You will surely discover additional sculptures tucked away in niches and along walkways.)

Old Westbury Gardens are not unknown in the New York area, so we suggest visiting on a weekday if you can. There is a moderate admission charge. (Holiday festivities are occasionally held at the estate.) You can pick up pamphlets and guides to the garden at the mansion.

INFORMATION

Old Westbury Gardens are located at 710 Old Westbury Road. Their hours are 10:00 A.M. to 5:00 P.M. every day except Tuesday, May through December. Wheelchair accessible. Telephone: (516) 333-0048

DIRECTIONS

From New York City, take the Midtown Tunnel to the Long Island Expressway to Exit 39S (Glen Cove Road). Continue east on the service road of the expressway 1 2/10 miles to Old Westbury Road, the first road on the right. Continue 1/4 mile to the garden entrance on your left. (Also reachable by Long Island Railroad to Westbury from Pennsylvania Station in New York, and by taxi from the Westbury station.)

7

The Cloisters: Walking Down Medieval Garden Paths

New York City, New York

Among the particularly magical parts of the Cloisters (the Metropolitan's medieval-style museum in northern Manhattan) are the gardens. While the pleasures of visiting the museum's medieval architecture and seeing its exquisite collection of fine art from the Middle Ages may be well known to New York's museumgoers, its gardens are in themselves well worth a special trip. The arcades of five cloisters have been reconstructed with the original stones and integrated into the museum's architecture; four cloisters surround their own unusual gardens. These spots are extraordinarily evocative; in fact, it is hard to believe you have to exit into the twentieth century when you leave. Though they are small, as gardens go, they are so filled with architectural, sculptural, and botanical interest that you might spend many hours walking round and round, or dreamily sitting on a bench imagining you are in thirteenth-century France, perhaps, or a member of a twelfth-century Cistercian order. Dimly heard medieval music sounds as you walk, and of course, the art treasures of this distant past await you in the stone-walled rooms of the museum.

Two of the cloisters (square-columned walkways that once

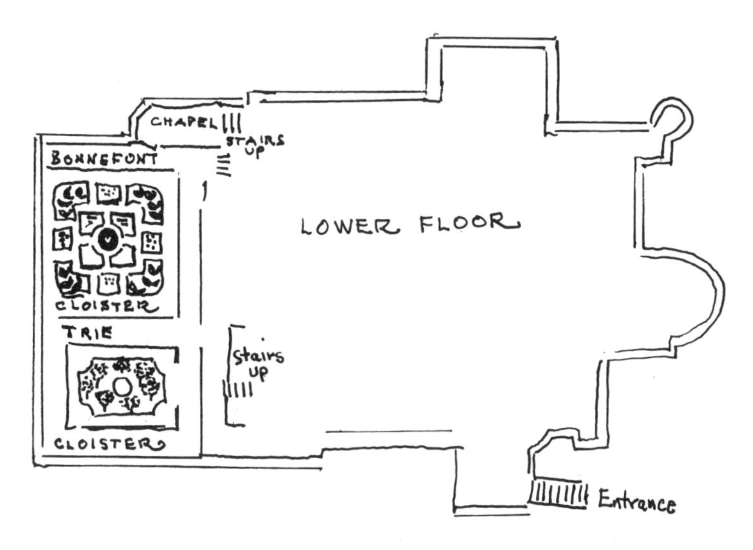

THE CLOISTERS

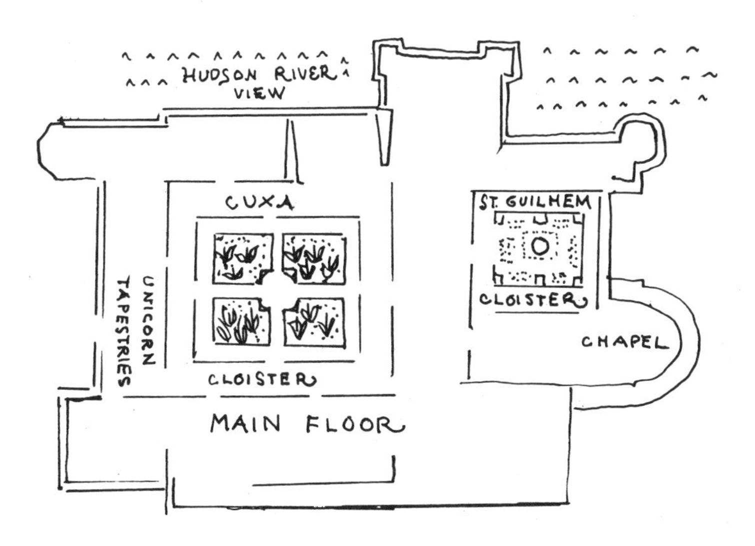

were parts of monasteries) are enjoyable to visit even out of garden season, for they are in covered areas and are kept flowering throughout the winter. All four of the cloister gardens are at their best in late spring and early summer, of course, when the flowers are blooming, the herbs bright and green, the espaliers leafy on their trellises. The following thumbnail descriptions should give you an idea of what to expect from each of these (chronologically listed) gardenwalks.

The earliest cloister is Saint-Guilhem le Desert. Formerly part of a French abbey that dates back to a Benedictine order in 804 A.D. Saint-Guilhem Cloister was built in 1206. Its stone pillars are topped by capitals (the decorative carved tops) whose designs are based on the spiny leaf of the acanthus plant. But there are many additional patterns carved on these columns, including a wonderful series of faces, flowers, entwined vines, and elegant foliage. There are small holes drilled into these designs in intricate honeycomb patterns, and no two columns seem the same.

Some of the sculptural decoration can be traced to ancient Roman design (still in evidence in southern France). This cloister surrounds an indoor garden that is planted fully in early spring. When we saw it last in winter, the flowers were potted and neatly arranged. The architectural details occasionally seem to imitate the very shapes of the leaves and flowers.

Almost directly across the central room from the Saint-Guilhem le Desert Cloister is the wonderful Saint Michel de Cuxa Cloister, a beautiful spot both in winter and in spring and summer, when it is ablaze with flowers. This cloister was in a Benedictine abbey first built in 878, though the cloister itself is from the twelfth century. From an area northeast of the Pyrenees, it forms the central part of the framework of the Cloister museum and is appropriately gracious and inviting. Its original function as a communal place for monks to walk, meditate, read, or take part in processionals can be readily imagined. The lovely stone walks surrounded by archways and columns open onto a sunlit garden of individual bedded flowers and plants. Each column is carved with typically medieval gargoyles, two-headed animals, or two-bodied monsters. You will want to spend time examining this garden and its cloisters, and perhaps sitting on a bench enjoying the ambience of quiet and beauty.

On the lower level of the museum you'll find the Bonnefont Cloister, a purely outdoor garden walkway. Its origins are in the south of France, near Toulouse. The cloister, with its slender graceful columns in rows of twos, comes from the late thirteenth-early fourteenth century. Cistercian monks once walked through these cloisters, and the very simple design of the architecture and limited amount of sculptural pattern represent their ascetism. (Decoration was not meant to draw attention away from devotion to duty and God.) Of particular garden interest here is the herb garden, a favorite among New Yorkers. More than 250 species of plants that were grown in the Middle Ages are cultivated in this outdoor space. In the center is a charming little well. The herbs are grown in raised planting beds with fences around them. Among our particular favorites here are the trained espaliers, growing against lattices in the sunlight. Anyone with an interest in gardening will find this cloister irresistible.

Finally, the fourth cloister, also on the lower level, is the Trie Cloister, from a Carmelite building in the Bigorre region of southern France. Reassembled with parts of several other cloisters, this small outdoor garden arcade is of particular interest if you look at the Unicorn Tapestries in the museum. The garden contains samples of the very plants woven into the design of tha tapestries some five centuries ago. (Information at the cloisters will identify them for you.) Part of the charm of this garden is the sight of the red tile roof surrounding it and the fruit trees set among the flowers. This garden, of course, is also only cultivated during growing months.

Though obviously you will get more pleasure out of this medieval garden walk in the growing season, even in wintertime it is nice to wander about the unkempt cloisters outdoors, to see the view of the Hudson, and to contemplate the beauty of the architecture and sculptural designs in the indoor gardens.

Among the many treasures you will want to enjoy in the museum while you are there are the Unicorn Tapestries, the stained glass in the Boppard Room, the wonderful altarpiece by the fifteenth-century painter Robert Campin, and our particular favorites, the medieval wood sculptures. Children, by the way, will enjoy this walk; there are numerous crenellated walls, dark staircases, impressive and picturesque statues that they'll love, and even medieval playing cards on display.

A visit to the Cloisters is perhaps the closest you can get to being in France while in Manhattan. We found the combination of art, history, and flowering plants an irresistible delight.

Many events of interest are held at the Cloisters; among them are gallery talks on such subjects as medieval imagery, tapestries, gardens of the Middle Ages, and colors in use in Medieval France. There are many concerts of medieval music played on early instruments. You will also find demonstrations of how medieval art was made, including such techniques as enameling and miniature painting. There is a guide to the gardens in which each plant is labeled and described. If you feel the need for additional exercise, you might wish to leave the Cloisters by way of Fort Tryon Park and walk south through this very pleasant park with its terrific views of the Hudson and New Jersey's palisades.

INFORMATION

Obviously, the best time to visit is during the week, when the museum is less crowded (although you might meet groups of school children). Hours: Tuesday–Sunday, 9:30–5:15, from March–October; Tuesday–Sunday, 9:30–4:45, from November–February. Closed New Year's Day, Thanksgiving, and Christmas. There is a fee. Wheelchair accessible. Guided tours available. Telephone: (212) 923-3700

DIRECTIONS

Subway: A train to 190th Street and Overlook Terrace; exit by elevator and walk through the park.
Bus: M4 Madison Avenue (Fort Tryon Park—The Cloisters).
Car: West Side Drive (Henry Hudson Parkway) north to first exit after George Washington Bridge. Follow signs. Parking on premises.

8

Aspet: Home and Studio of Augustus Saint-Gaudens

Cornish, New Hampshire

If your idea of the nineteenth century artist living in the depth of a city in a dreadful Bohemian garret needs changing, visit the home and studio of Augustus Saint-Gaudens. Now a National Historic site complete with Park Rangers and one of the most beautiful landscapes imaginable, Aspet, the artist's summer place and eventual year-round home, is a rarely visited treasure. You may come away thinking that life as one of America's most famous sculptors must have been heavenly.

The National Park Service has made this memorial to Saint-Gaudens an elegant, tasteful, and fascinating place to visit. Though Saint-Gaudens' own experiences there were not so universally glamorous and moneyed as they now appear (the docent told us that several disastrous studio fires and a $30,000 loan to keep the place going were among the less glorious facts of Aspet's past), this estate shows off his art and architecture in a noble fashion. From the distant vistas of fields and mountains, to the charmingly columned and arbored studios, to the delicately set sculptures along garden paths, this is how we would like to imagine an illustrious artist's estate.

The site of Aspet is in rural Cornish, New Hampshire, just

beyond the longest covered bridge in the nation. It crosses the Connecticut River from Vermont at Windsor. Nearby, a perfectly kept roadway into the deep woods takes you to Aspet. Despite its original use as a posting house along a traveled route, the house and its surroundings seemed to us wonderfully remote, like some Shangri-la amid the picturesque New England countryside. The large property includes a number of studios in addition to the sculptor's home, formal gardens, a deep wooded ravine, and enough fields and lawns to satisfy even a walker without a taste for sculpture. A striking view of nearby Mount Ascutney adds to the vista. But the art is, of course, the featured attraction, magnificently displayed with architecture and nature as its allies.

Augustus Saint-Gaudens was one of America's premier artists and probably its most beloved nineteenth century sculptor. Born in 1848 in Dublin to a French shoemaker's family from the small village of Aspet in the Pyrenees, Augustus was brought to the United States as a baby. At thirteen he was apprenticed to a cameo cutter. (And, in fact, his large bronze cameos later became a staple of his work; many are displayed at the estate.) At nineteen he left for Europe to study art, working as a cameo cutter in Paris and Rome to support himself. In Paris he experimented with naturalistic representation and the modeling of surfaces; in Rome he studied the works of Donatello and delicate low relief.

At twenty-seven he returned home and began his American career. He worked briefly with John LaFarge (as a mural painter), and began his lifelong friendships with the architects Stanford White and Charles McKim. They eventually collaborated in many projects, some of which can be seen at Aspet.

It was the commission in 1876 to create a statue commemorating Admiral David Farragut that brought Saint-Gaudens lasting recognition and success. The statue was exhibited in

Paris, cast in bronze and placed in Madison Square in New York. Set upon Stanford White's unusual pedestal, Saint-Gaudens' unconventional, powerful figure of the admiral made him a celebrity. (A cast of this work is prominently displayed at Aspet.)

Saint-Gaudens' naturalistic approach contrasted with the smooth, controlled surfaces and contours of neoclassical sculpture that had been in vogue. By 1880 he had become an acknowledged leader of American sculptors in an era in which the memorial statue was a necessity in every city square. Other artists joined him in rejecting academicism; in 1878 he was a founder of the Society of American Artists, which sought to free both painting and sculpture from academic and banal styles of portraiture.

His commemorative statues of famous people (including Abraham Lincoln) were in great demand and are familiar images to us today. But perhaps his best known and most beloved work—beautifully displayed at Aspet—was his venture into a more emotional style: his *Adams Memorial.* This grieving, hooded figure was arguably the most original and haunting sculpture yet achieved by an American.

Saint-Gaudens became a widely respected teacher and leader of other artists. In 1885 after he bought the old staging inn that was to become Aspet, Cornish became the center of an artists' colony that grew up about him. (Legend has it that a friend persuaded him to go to New England in the summertime; he was then at work on an important Lincoln portrait and was told that he would find among the natives of New Hampshire many "Lincoln-shaped" men to use for models.)

Aspet became a center both for sculptors and other creative people; Saint-Gaudens' salon attracted poets, novelists, journalists, and actors. You'll find a flyer describing the Cornish Colony's illustrious members at Aspet. The artists included sculptors Frederick MacMonnies, Philip Martiny, and

James Earle Fraser; among the painters were George deForest Brush, Thomas Deming and Maxfield Parrish.

For some twenty-two years Saint-Gaudens worked at Aspet, adding continually to the estate by building new studios and gardens and redesigning the old. During these full years he created some of his most famous works, advised presidents and museums, and won numerous international prizes and awards. (Agreeably, the displays at Aspet are devoted to his art rather than to his illustrious life as important artist.)

Aspet became a National Historic site in 1965, the first home of an artist to be so designated. (The second is Weir Farm in Connecticut.) Like other National Park sites, this one provides guided tours of the house and grounds, but you can also wander on your own throughout the estate (but you cannot enter the house unaccompanied).

Begin your visit at the sculptor's home. Here, in a perfect white New England house with a grand columned veranda shaded by grape leaves, you can sit and contemplate the vista (or wait for a house tour).

The house, which dates to about 1800, is small roomed and Victorian within, hardly reflecting the grandeur of Saint-Gaudens' sculptural conceptions. Deep peach and rose-colored drapes and shades, a large faded tapestry, and dark Victorian furniture set the tone. A few small, curious paintings enliven the interior—one by his friend and colleague architect Stanford White, another by the sculptor's wife.

The spectacular veranda was added to the house, and is its most inviting feature. Its classical columns and magnificent view conjure visions of the Cornish Colony seated in the prevailing westerly breeze and discussing art and literature one hundred years ago.

But to begin your tour, leave the veranda from the far steps and make your way to the gardens below. Saint-Gaudens had a taste for landscape design, white marble paths, and formal gardens. Of particular note are the rare clumps of mature white birches which are carefully maintained, and the individually designed rectangular flower gardens. Each part of the estate has its own plan with borders and hedges of pine or hemlock. Small sculptured heads appear above the boxwood here and there. There are pools, fountains that shoot jets of water through the mouths of fish and turtles (designed by the sculptor), and marble benches for the proper contemplation of it all. (The white bench decorated with figures of Pan playing his pipes is, however, the work of Augustus' brother Louis, also a sculptor of note.)

Your next stop is the Little Studio, an enchanting building that was once a hay barn. Transformed for Saint-Gaudens into a romantic workplace, the Little Studio reminds us of the sculptor's fascination with the images of antiquity. George Babb, an associate of Stanford White, redesigned the old barn into an Italianate classical structure. It has brilliant white columns now ornamented with clinging vines, contrasting with a rose-red wall (described as "Pompeiian red") and a frieze that copies the figures of the Parthenon.

Inside the Little Studio, which was the sculptor's personal workplace, is a charming room filled with natural light. It contains small Saint-Gaudens works, including low-relief portraits, many books, and a small corner where a twenty-eight minute video of the sculptor's life is shown. (This seems to be the only modern-tech touch except for lawn mowers droning on the vast grounds.) Another room houses a discreet shop of memorabilia and books on the sculptor. The Little Studio is as pretty a place to picture an artist creating as you can imagine, but today there is little sign that he actually worked there. (How to present a "working" studio to the public is an ongoing debate in preservationist circles.) The Little Studio also presents a series of chamber music concerts.

On leaving this building, follow the path toward the *Adams Memorial* in its own garden, grandly surrounded by a square hedge and plantings. Arguably Saint-Gaudens' most stunning work, this is a cast of the original in Washington. The shrouded, seated figure was commissioned by Henry Adams on the death of his wife in 1885. It is not a portrait but a symbol of mourning which brought American sculpture to a new depth of emotion, anticipating expressionism by many years.

When the British novelist John Galsworthy saw it, he remarked that it gave him more pleasure than anything else he had seen in America, commenting, "That great greenish bronze figure of [a] seated woman within the hooding folds of her ample cloak seemed to carry [one] down to the bottom of [one's] soul."

Through the hedgerow and along the birch-lined pathway you'll see the bowling green, where the family and friends played lawn bowls. Next you'll come to a well-known portrait head of Abraham Lincoln and then to the *Shaw Memorial.* This large bronze bas-relief commemorates the Fifty-fourth black regiment from Massachusetts in the Civil War. (This is also a cast of the original, which stands in the Boston Commons.) Saint-Gaudens worked for fourteen years on this major sculpture. It is surrounded by a white grape arbor in a sun-dappled garden.

Nearby is a carriage barn filled with highly polished carriages and sleighs. (Saint-Gaudens enjoyed tobogganing and other sports at Aspet.)

Returning to the path, bear left across the open lawn to the Gallery. This comparatively modern building houses both Saint-Gaudens' sculpture and pretty gardens, as well as a changing exhibit of contemporary painting, sculpture and photography. In the atrium of the gallery there is a reflecting pool. The sculptor originally had built a studio for his plaster molder and areas for his assistants on the site; it burned in 1904 with the loss of many works in progress, sketchbooks, and correspondence. Its replacement was also destroyed by fire in 1944.

Among the high points of Saint-Gaudens' works in the gallery are his famous massive statue called *The Puritan,* and a particularly appealing wall-size bas-relief of the ailing Robert Louis Stevenson, bedridden, but nonetheless a romantic figure. The gallery for today's artists is a nice bright space that was showing the work of Louis Iselin at our last visit. (Needless to say, his sculptures looked shockingly modern in this nineteenth century environment.)

Outside the gallery is the *Farragut Base,* the original stone pedestal for the monumental and influential statue that brought Saint-Gaudens such celebrity. Designed in collaboration with Stanford White, it is indeed impressive with its rough texture and free form.

From here, follow signs to the Ravine Studio, which Saint-Gaudens used occasionally. This is still a real and well-used studio where a contemporary sculptor is generally at work and will welcome you as part of the interpretative program of the Historic Site; the artist is in residence in season Fridays to Mondays from 9:00 A.M. to 4:30 P.M. It is a nice touch to see sculpture in process after so much finished work.

The estate also includes a dramatic and rather steep descent into a forested ravine. (A nature trail guide is available where you park.) If you choose to take this walk you will find it exceptionally beautiful, but be sure you are wearing proper shoes for a climb!

The path eventually will bring you to the bottom of the great field in front of the house where the Cornish Colony had a Greek-style, columned temple erected in 1905 to celebrate twenty years of Saint-Gaudens' residence at Aspet. It became the family burial place.

This is but a thumbnail sketch of the many pleasures to be found at Aspet. A true student of sculpture might spend a long day noting the many works of art—some almost hidden among the shrubbery—while a nature buff could hike the paths of Aspet for an equally long time. You will choose your own pace here, perhaps resting on a marble bench in front of a well-known statue, or examining the many small bas-reliefs on Saint-Gaudens' studio walls. Whatever style is yours, this is a walk to savor.

INFORMATION

The Saint-Gaudens National Historic Site is open daily from the last weekend in May through October 31. The buildings are open from 8:30 A.M. to 4:30 P.M. daily and the grounds from 8:00 A.M. until dark. There is an inexpensive admission fee for persons over sixteen. Partly wheelchair accessible. The mailing address is RR 3, Box 73, Cornish, NH 03745; telephone: (603) 675-2175.

DIRECTIONS

From Boston take the Massachusetts Turnpike to Route 91 north to exit 8; take Route 131 East and go left onto Route 12A north. Aspet is located just off Route 12A in Cornish, New Hampshire; it is twelve miles north of Claremont, New Hampshire and two and a half miles north of the Covered Bridge at Windsor, Vermont.

9

A Brooklyn Delight: Botanical Garden Walk

Brooklyn, New York

The Brooklyn Botanic Garden at 1000 Washington Avenue is one of those surprises you happen upon in New York. In the midst of busy urban sprawl, around the corner from a dreary stretch of Flatbush Avenue (but very near the lovely Prospect Park), you enter the iron gates of the Brooklyn Botanic Garden. There you find yourself in an enchanting, colorful, and completely intriguing world of planned gardens, elegant walkways, weeping cherry trees, and the many sights and smells of the world's most inviting gardens. The area was reclaimed from a waste dump in 1910. It takes up some 50 acres (but seems actually much larger), and you can walk among them quite randomly, from the Japanese paths along a lake to the formal rose gardens, from the Shakespeare Garden to the excellent conservatories. As you will see in the description that follows there are many pleasures in these 50 acres, particularly if you take this outing in the spring.

Every season highlights a different area or style of garden, but surely April, May, and June are the most colorful times to come, when the ornamental trees, luxuriant roses, and many spring flowers are in bloom. But the rock garden is ablaze with flowers during the entire growing season, and the roses bloom with different species through September. A fragrance garden, labeled in Braille for the blind, is another fine section of the gardens; it, too, is open during the spring, summer, and fall.

All of the plants are labeled, and there are more than 12,000 of them. The conservatories and outdoor gardens among them include plants from almost every country in the world. If your taste is for literary references, you can enjoy the Shakespeare Garden, where plantings are related to passages from the Bard's works. If you want to meditate you might choose to sit along the banks of the Japanese Garden's lovely walkways. If you are a horticultural fan, there is a Local Flora section and many interesting displays of temperate, rain forest, and desert plants.

Sometimes described as "many gardens within a garden" (there are fourteen specialty gardens, many linked along a winding stream), the Brooklyn Botanic is one of the nicest places to spend a day in the city. (You can even eat in one of the gardens.) You'll find it a unique blending of intimacy and grandeur that brings to mind the fine gardens of England rather than the wilder acres of the Bronx Botanical Garden or Central Park.

At the two main entrances to the Botanic Garden (on Washington Avenue) you can pick up a very useful map, which will point you in the right direction. A good place to begin your walk is the Herb Garden, near the parking lot. This charming contoured plot contains over three hundred carefully labeled herbs that have been used for medicine and cooking since the Middle Ages. Intricate Elizabethan knots form an intriguing pattern amid the plantings and add a unique element to this garden. From here you can take a lower or upper walkway. The upper path will lead you to the Overlook, bordered by gingko trees and to the grassy terrace known as the Osbourne section, where a promenade of green lawns with stylishly shaped shrubs and freestanding columns await you. The pleasant, leafy lower lane will take you past groupings of peonies, crabapple trees, and wisterias to the Cherry Esplanade. We recommend you see this garden in late April or early May, when the deep pink blossoms of the Kwanzan cherry trees are a breathtaking dreamlike pastel. The trees are arranged in rows alongside tall, Norwegian maples whose dark red leaves create a wonderful contrast in color.

The adjacent Cranford Rose Garden, with its nine hundred varieties (over five thousand strong) is the third largest such garden in the country. In this acre of pure enchantment you can identify the roses and study them carefully or simply enjoy the overall quality of their rare beauty.

On the hillside behind a wooden fence is the Local Flora section, an unusual and less frequented garden. In these two

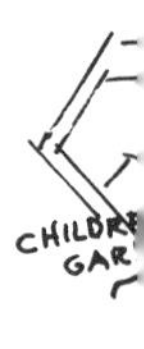

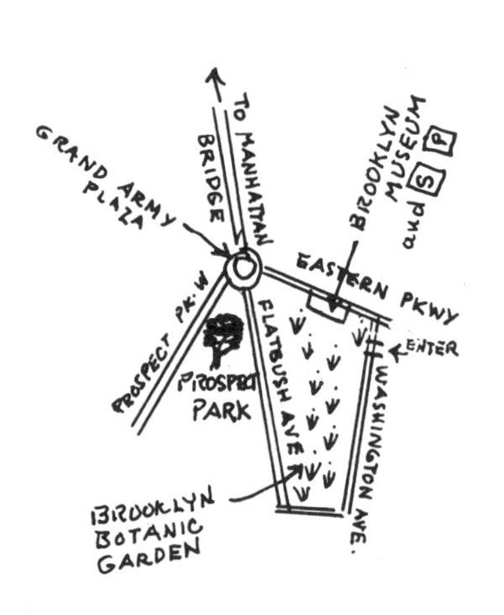

secluded acres the nine ecological zones found within a 100-mile radius of the Botanic Garden have been re-created in dioramalike form. Serpentine rock, dry meadow and stream, kettle pond, bog, pine barrens, wet meadow and stream, deciduous woodland, border mound, and limestone ledge habitats are displayed with their corresponding flora and rock formations. This rare outdoor classroom is meant for serious observers and nature lovers (school groups are not invited) who want to spend time carefully examining the 100 or so plant varieties indigenous to this area, such as the many ferns, phlox, grasses, magnolias, pines, rhododendrons, larches, oaks, heather, persimmon trees, mosses, and dogwoods found here. If you wish to study the plants further, you can pick up a guide called *Local Flora Section,* available at the bookstore, since the plants in this garden are not labeled.

From the Local Flora section walk down the hill, past the hedgewheel, a whimsical composition of eighteen different

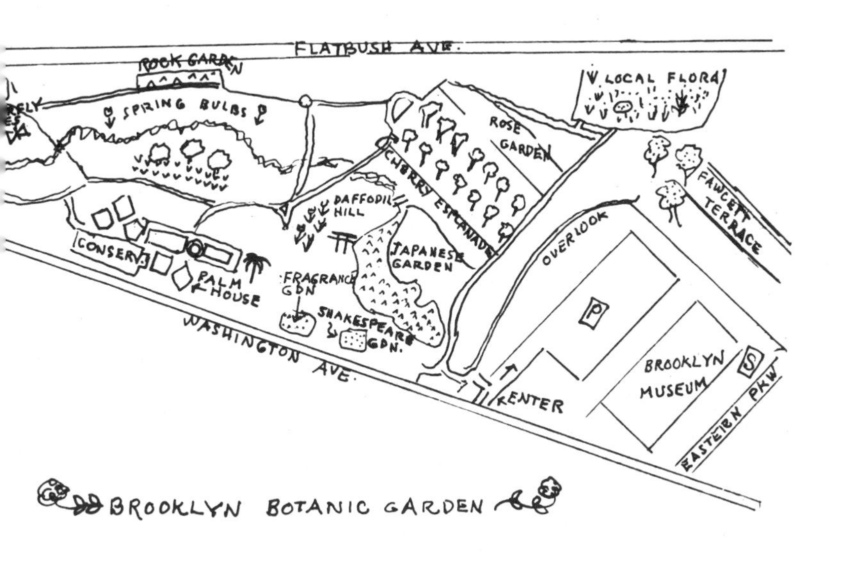

hedging plants (boxwoods, viburnum, holly, and yew) to the lovely rock garden on your right. Here, rounded glacial boulders define the site that is planted with contour evergreen shrubs, different types of ground cover, and flowering plants that provide a vivid palette of color for much of the year. Along the path are clumps of spring bulbs, honeysuckles, and forsythias. You'll walk past a bed of barberries that contains twenty varieties, from exotic bamboolike plants to delicate specimens with dainty red and yellow buds. A stream meanders by, flanked by weeping willows, adding to the effect of a romantic English garden.

Eventually you will come to the conservatory complex (called the Steinhardt Conservatory). Here, three new, beautifully designed greenhouses contain a rich collection of tropical, temperate, and desert plants, including some three thousand pounds of cacti and succulents brought from the Arizona desert. Throughout the year you can enjoy the wonderful flower displays as well as the permanent collection of palms, ferns, and exotic specimens that grace these pavilions. We particularly liked a grotto (in the Tropical Pavilion), carved out of granite, and filled with ferns, and the Aquatic House, containing two pools and various plants according to natural habitat. You can view the deeper pool from two perspectives: at the Aquatic House, where you look down on it, or from windows in the Exhibition Gallery on the lower floor, where these unusual aquatic plants can be examined from an angle people rarely see. One gallery is devoted to bonsai, and you can admire the prized collectors' items (some date from the 1920s) in their many varieties, from the most formal upright to surprisingly naturalistic styles. The curious and intricate art of dwarfing plants is carefully explained and described. The resulting "tray" gardens are real miniature versions—down to the last detail—of regular pines, bamboos, maples, or elms. While you are within the conservatories don't miss the Exhibition Gallery in the central lower level. It features horticultural displays and art exhibits relating to plants in an atriumlike space. On a recent visit we enjoyed seeing a show called "My Garden," a group of alabaster flowers in sensuous configurations by the English sculptor Diana Guest.

Outside the conservatories, next to two reflecting pools, is the elegant Victorian Palm House, once the main conservatory. This lovely old building (now used for special gatherings) adds a dash of turn-of-the-century glamour to the complex. Nearby is the Administration Building, the focus of the many educational and research programs conducted by the Botanic Garden. Workshops, lectures, exhibits, concerts, films, and classes on just about anything relating to plants are held here. In addition, there is an Herbarium (which includes some 250,000 dried plant specimens), a plant and book shop, and a horticultural reference library.

The Magnolia Plaza, just outside, a terrace where over eighty magnolia trees bloom in May, is formally designed with concentric circular and linear paths. The path to your right (as you face the plaza) will take you to the Fragrance Garden, a delightful, intimate spot that is a pleasure to the senses. Here, plants labeled in Braille can also be identified through touching and smelling.

You'll find the Shakespeare Garden off to the east of the pathway. Here the tiny signs not only identify the plants but indicate Shakespeare's references to each flower. This is great fun for those of us who remember our plays and sonnets, and for those who don't—for there is a guide available at the bookshop. It also includes a full map, noting where to find such flowers and apt quotations as "I think the king is but a man, as I am. The violet smells to him as it doth to me," *(Henry V),* "For though the camomile, the more it is trodden on, the faster it grows, yet youth, the more it is wasted, the sooner it wears," *(Henry IV),* and "What's in a name? That which we call a rose by any other name would smell as sweet," *(Romeo and Juliet).* In addition to the many plants of note, the garden itself is laid out in a charming, orderly fashion surrounded by a serpentine wall. An oval brick path, a fountain, and a bench contribute to the impression of an English cottage garden of Shakespeare's times. Be sure to pick up the guide with its many nice illustrations of Elizabethan gardens before you get to this pretty spot, for it will add to your pleasure.

And, finally, you will come to what is arguably the highlight of a visit to the Botanic Garden: the exquisite Japanese Hill and Pond Garden. Designed by Tokeo Shiota in 1914, this prize garden reflects the religious and natural symbolism inherent in Japanese gardens in which various elements are combined to form a harmonious blend of beauty and peace. The Japanese garden is regarded as a holy site, as well as a place for quiet reflection where the visitor can be at one with nature. And, incredibly, in the heart of Brooklyn, one of the city's most populous areas, this garden provides just that. Walk past the massive Komatsu stone lantern (dating from the seventeenth century) and enter the circular viewing pavilion, which welcomes the visitor, as it represents the home of the host. Before you is the breathtaking pond surrounded by a magical tableau of hillside cascades, grottoes, paths through shaded pine groves, and carefully planted shrubberies. A brilliant red torri, a wooden gateway indicating the presence of a nearby temple, stands in the pond, its dramatic image mirrored in the reflecting water. In spring, flowering quince, tree peonies, and weeping Higan cherry trees add even more splashes of color. As you view this rare spot, you will be eager to wander about and explore the garden. Your walk will take you around the pond, through winding paths flanked with junipers, hollies, and yews that are shaped like sculptures, flowering shrubs and trees, past the cavelike grottoes and up the hill to the Shinto shrine found within a quiet grove of evergreens.

Although the garden is relatively small, it is beautifully designed to give the impression of spaciousness as well as intimacy. To leave the Japanese Garden you must retrace your steps to the entrance, which will put you near the Herb Garden from where you began your circular walk.

INFORMATION

Spring is the most spectacular time to visit, although there are blooming periods from late winter to November. Try to go on weekdays when it's less crowded. A Cherry Blossom Festival is held here annually from late April into early May.

The Botanic Garden is open Tuesday–Friday (May–August), 8–6, and weekends and holidays, 10–6; from September to April it is open Tuesday–Friday, 8–4:30, and on weekends and holidays, 10–4:30. There is no entrance fee. The Conservatory's hours are Tuesday–Friday, 10–4 and weekends and holidays, 11–4. There is a small entrance fee. Wheelchair accessible. For information, call (718) 622-4433.

DIRECTIONS

Subway: #2 or #3 to Eastern Parkway station or D or Q train to Prospect Park station.

Car: Take the Manhattan Bridge, whose continuation in Brooklyn is Flatbush Avenue; stay on Flatbush all the way to the Grand Army Plaza at Prospect Park, and take the rotary three-fourths of the way around to Eastern Parkway, which borders the park. The Botanic Gardens are immediately after the Central Library building. There is a large parking area (small fee).

10

Rockland Lake: An Off-Season Lake Walk

Congers, New York

The Rockland Lake walk is a pleasant circular three-mile jaunt along the edge of the water. The lake lies within Rockland Lake State Park, 588 acres of somewhat developed parklands with sports and picnic facilities. During busy summer weekends the park is crowded and noisy with the sounds of blaring radios. For this reason we recommend this walk off-season or on weekdays, when it is wonderfully peaceful. This is a flat, easy walk that will also appeal to bikers and nature lovers.

Rockland Lake is a post-glacial lake, once famous for the excellent quality of the ice produced here before refrigeration. In fact, its ice was exported not only to nearby areas, but also as far away as the Caribbean. The remnants of ice houses used to store the ice can still be seen in the park.

Although you are never really far away from "civilization," this lakeside walk is still bucolic. Willows line the path; there are peaceful views of fishermen in rowboats, surrounded by water lilies. There are ducks, swans, and geese everywhere, encouraged by families with children who bring food for

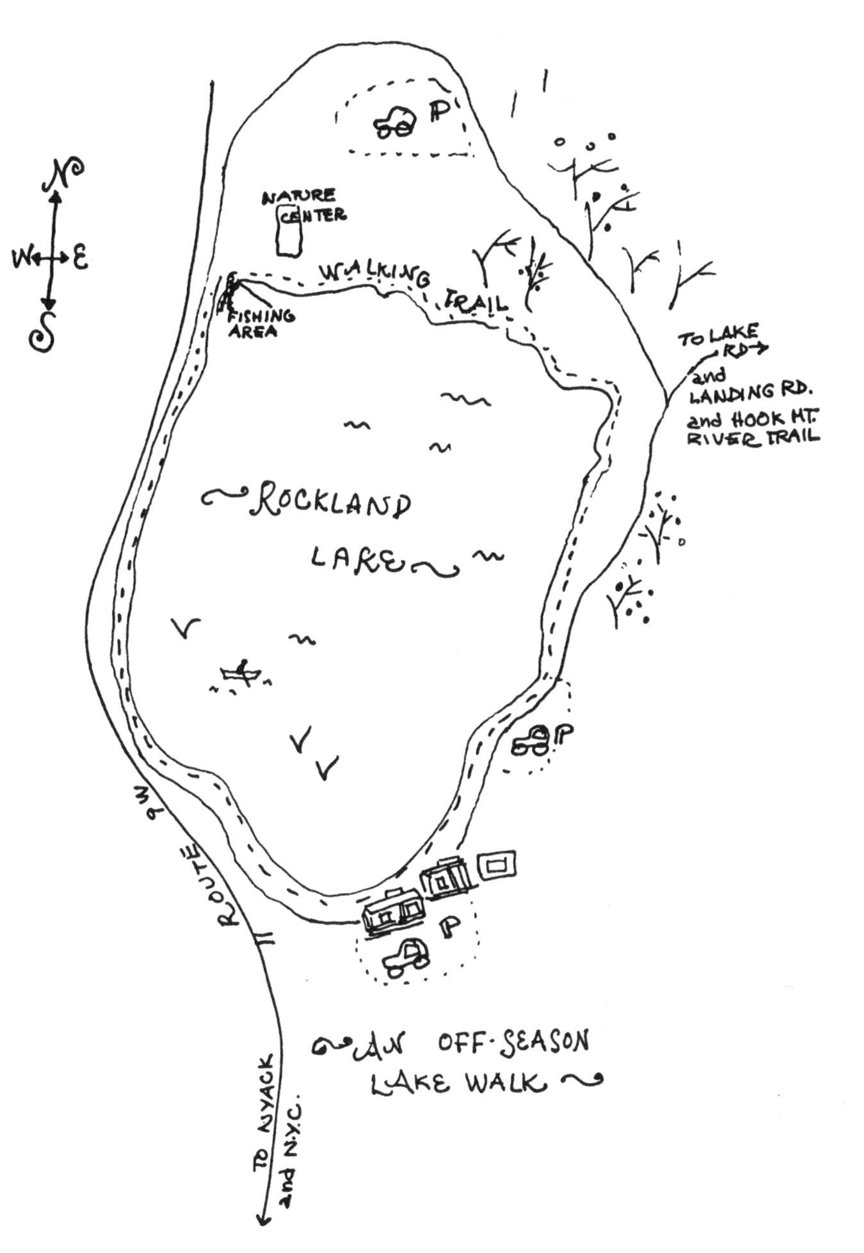
N
W
E
S
NATURE CENTER
WALKING TRAIL
FISHING AREA
TO LAKE RD
and LANDING RD.
and HOOK MT. RIVER TRAIL
ROCKLAND LAKE
P
ROUTE 9W
TO NYACK and N.Y.C.
AN OFF-SEASON LAKE WALK

them. In the fall you might see mute swans, originally domesticated birds from Europe, that live in pairs and sometimes reach the age of 100.

Park either near the swimming pool and bathhouse (for a small fee) or by the fishing and comfort station where parking is free. You can't miss the path: in addition to being a footpath, it is a bike trail and marked as such. It doesn't matter in which direction you start, or at what point you begin your walk, as you will eventually come back to your starting point.

Take in your surroundings: the many wonderful wildflowers and shrubs that bloom along the path during June, the trees reflected in the lake, and the sounds of birds overhead. You might be able to identify some of the following species: downy woodpecker, song sparrow, red-winged blackbird, tree swallow, mockingbird, yellow warbler, Baltimore oriole, gold finch, catbird, and swamp sparrow.

Eventually you will come to the nature center, a smallish wooden structure at the north side of the lake. There you can see displays of live snakes, toads, frogs, fish, and salamanders indigenous to these parts. From the nature center there are two marshy trails (totaling about .5 mile) which take you through a woodland swamp. You walk atop a boardwalk through dark woods, past a variety of plants that are identified on markers. You'll see spicebush (early settlers made tea from its fragrant twigs and leaves), red maples, white ash, red oak, tulip trees, swamp loosestrife, ferns, and red osiers. It is a pleasant surprise to come upon a clearing and good view of the lake, from where the second trail begins. This lakeside bog trail, a shaded leafy walk with a canopy of shrubs overhead, takes you past wild flowering bushes, swamp azaleas, arrowwood (used by Indians for arrow shafts), high-bush blueberry, and winterberry. There is a lovely second lookout point where you might want to pause briefly to enjoy the scenery. The path leads back to the main lakeside walk, where you can continue, if you like.

INFORMATION

Avoid the weekends of July and August! Otherwise, this is an all-season walk. If you plan to do more than walk—you can fish, ice skate, row a boat, or watch for birds—you should check to see when those activities are available. Birders should go between March and October; there is good ice skating and ice fishing on cold winter days; and you can rent a rowboat, rain or shine, from March to the end of October. Winter is especially nice if there's not a cold wind blowing.

This is an outing for people of any age or physical ability. Seniors will enjoy ambling along this mostly shaded path at a leisurely pace; children will like feeding the waterfowl; nature lovers can look for various species of flora and fauna. Others might just like to be in a quiet setting with pleasant views at every turn.

If you are a birder, bring binoculars. Bring along a picnic; there are several lakeside picnic tables, but you will also find plenty of shade trees to sit under or lookout points from which to enjoy the view. Wheelchair accessible. Telephone: (914) 786-2701.

DIRECTIONS

From west side of Manhattan: West Side Highway, George Washington Bridge, Palisades Parkway, exit 4, north on Route 9W. Go about 9 miles on Route 9W. Access to Rockland State Park is off Route 9W and is well marked, and there are several parking areas. From east side of Manhattan: FDR Drive, Harlem River Drive, George Washington Bridge, and follow same directions as above.

11

Sculpture Gardens at PepsiCo: An Inviting Park on Corporate Grounds

Purchase, New York

We have no hesitation in inviting you to take this walk; it is truly one of our favorites both with and without children in tow. You may wonder how PepsiCo—so well known for its mainstream popular culture advertising—would find itself in a book about public art and gardens. But you are in for a wonderful surprise. While there are many corporate art collections in America, few are available to the public to enjoy with the scale, variety, and quality of the Donald M. Kendall Sculpture Gardens at PepsiCo.

A walking tour of these 112 acres (more an estate than a garden in the traditional sense) will introduce you to some forty-two major works of sculpture, as well as to a shining example of how a corporation can enhance its surroundings and bring art to people outside of a museum. The former CEO of the company, Donald M. Kendall, conceived the idea and was active in collecting the sculpture to provide "an environment that encourages creativity and reflects essential qualities of corporate success." (While you may find that few of these works of art seem to relate in any way to corporate success, the sense of creativity is indeed all around you.)

In 1970 Edward Durell Stone's massive building was opened on this exquisite site—formerly a polo field. The building (which is not open to the public) is made up of seven square blocks that form three courtyard gardens around a central fountain. The architect's son laid out the surrounding acreage of rolling green terrain; there are fields, pathways, a lake, distinctive trees, flower gardens, fountains—and everywhere you look—sculpture.

The gardens themselves were planned by the internationally known landscape designer Russell Page. Each piece of art is carefully placed in relation to its surroundings, so that each knoll or valley provides a gentle setting for its work of art. There are both formal gardens—where smaller pieces of sculpture are surrounded with clipped hedges and precisely groomed plantings—and vast fields—where monumental examples of contemporary sculpture stand starkly against the horizon. There is a lake and well-tended woodland. This park is so carefully designed and maintained that even the parking lots are concealed by plantings, and an army of gardeners seems to be always at work. (A list of some of the most interesting trees and plantings appears at the end of this chapter.)

To begin your walk, leave your car in one of the hidden parking lots (to which discreet signs direct you). No appointment is necessary, but check the hours listed below. You will seldom find this vast place crowded. After you park, you'll go to the Visitor Center, pick up a numbered map, and enter the "Golden Path"—a nice, winding walkway through the entire acreage. (You may wander on your own if you prefer, or stay on the path and follow the map, which identifies all works of art.)

1. As you come to the fork in the path, go to your right. The first sculpture, just to the left of the path, is Alexander Calder's *Hats Off,* a giant work in orange-red metal, unmistakably Calder's. It is set against a backdrop of white fir and

Colorado blue spruce, bringing its brilliant color vividly to life.

2. Also to the left of the path is Jean Dubuffet's painted black and white abstract work *Kiosque Evide* (Figure 29). This 1985 sculpture by the renowned French artist does look like some fantastic kind of kiosk with its whimsical shapes and painted designs. Dubuffet described his works in this style not as sculptures but as "unleashed graphisms, drawings which extend and expand in space."

3. A little farther, also to your left, is a work by Arnaldo Pomodoro called *Grande Disco,* a variation on the form of the globe—eaten away by some mysterious forces. (Another Pomodoro work—and one of the major sculptures of the entire collection—is described below.)

4. Leave the path and walk left toward the building entrance to see a work by the well-known David Smith. This piece, called *Cube Totem Seven and Six,* is set just in front of the trellis to the giant headquarters building. You will no doubt recognize Smith's style in this delightful shiny metal work. (In fact, one of the characteristics of this sculpture collection is that each work is highly typical of its artist's style; you may enjoy identifying the works, if you are familiar with contemporary sculpture, without benefit of this guide.)

5. and 6. On the terrace in front of you, you'll find works by two twentieth century Italian masters. First, you'll see Marino Marini's charming *Horse and Rider.* Now somewhat of a "classic," Marini's signature horse and rider images are familiar, but always a pleasure to see anew. Also on the terrace are two Alberto Giacometti statues: *Standing Woman I and II,* their tall, thin figures sharply defined against the building's wall.

7. Auguste Rodin's *Eve* is perhaps the most traditional work on this walk, but it is interesting to see the origins of

contemporary sculpture in this lovely 1881 work. It is charmingly set among holly trees and shrubbery.

8. One of the most interesting works is Max Ernst's *Capricorn,* to the right of the path. Don't miss this surrealistic group of figures with animal parts suggesting fish, a cow, and birds.

(Here is an opportunity to visit the courtyard gardens that contain ten additional works of art. You can either enter the gateway at this juncture, or leave them for the end. They are described as numbers 33 to 42.)

9. One of today's leading sculptors is represented next; in a kind of garden area to your left you'll find Kenneth Snelson's *Mozart II.* This is a giant aluminum construction of geometric shapes and wires, a most contemporary tribute to Mozart.

10. Go back to the path and go left at the fork, near the building's walls. Here you'll see George Segal's *Three People on Four Benches,* a characteristically superrealistic work that may remind you of PepsiCo's workers relaxing during their lunch hour break.

11. Claes Oldenburg's *Giant Trowel II* is one of the most memorable sights at PepsiCo. In fact, it is so startling against its background of pine and dogwood trees that you blink to see if the giant spade is really there, digging into the green earth.

12. Moving farther along the path you'll next see George Rickey's *Double L Eccentric Gyratory II,* a typical Rickey work made up of stainless steel windmill-like blades that shift gently in the breeze.

13. and 14. Here, on the edge of the cultivated lawn area, and in front of a wooded section you'll come to Tony Smith's abstract *Duck* and Richard Erdman's *Passage.*

15. and 16. David Wynne's *The Dancers* is close to the en-

trance to the park, near an area called the stream garden, as is Art Price's *Birds of Welcome,* a rather folksy, but contemporary work that reminded us of Pennsylvania Dutch design.

17., 18. and 19. Also nearby are *The Search* by Victor Salmones; another David Wynne figure piece, *Dancer with Bird;* and William Crovello's *Katana.* These works are all surrounded by shrubbery and little woodsy walkways, in contrast to those on the terraces or open fields.

20. Some way past these works, to the left of the path, you'll come upon a fascinating work in the collection: Judith Brown's 1982 sculpture *Caryatids.* This is an interesting post-modern work which is reminiscent of ancient art—using old car parts in a highly contemporary manner. Don't miss this impression of crumbling ruins made of steel bits.

21., 22. and 23. Gidon Graetz is represented by *Composition in Stainless Steel No. 1,* which you'll find near the building on your left, while *Personnage,* a 1970 work by the "old" master, Joan Miró, is up on the terrace near the lily pond. (Don't miss this delightful garden spot with its perennial flower border and water lily pool. Here also is a charming pavilion inspired by eighteenth century English landscape design—and it is a perfect place for a quick rest.) Nearby is Robert Davidson's *Frog;* you'll see a more imposing work by this sculptor later on.

24. Next you'll come to one of the most memorable and defining works in the sculpture park: Arnaldo Pomodoro's *Triad,* a dramatic group of three modern, but ancient-looking, columns set starkly against the landscape.

25. and 26. The well-known British sculptor Barbara Hepworth is also represented with a typical work in this collection. Her *Meridien,* a 1959 piece, is to the left of the path near Bret Price's *Big Scoop.*

27. and 28. Next you'll find the works of two of the most often mentioned sculptors in our book: Isamu Noguchi and

Louise Nevelson. Both have defined contemporary sculpture in our time, in very different ways. Noguchi's work, *Energy Void,* is a characteristically formalistic work; Nevelson's *Celebration II* is a dark collection of geometric metal forms set in soft ground cover amid a stand of copper beech trees that reflect the color of the sculpture.

29. You have now reached the lake. In your walk around it you'll see several of the major works in the collection. First is Robert Davidson's three giant totems that will remind you of northwest coast native American carvings. This work, appropriately called *Totems,* stands out by its audacity, bright colors, and dramatic design.

30. and 31. Another contemporary work, Asmundur Sveinsson's *Through the Sound Barrier* is also next to the circular path around the lake. And at the intersection of the lake path and your original entrance to the grounds is one of the most beloved sculptures (particularly by children), David Wynne's realistic *Grizzly Bear.*

32. The last work on the grounds is Henry Moore's *Double Oval,* which sits on the edge of the lake as a splendid monument to contemporary art.

33.–42. If you haven't already detoured to the courtyards, you will now wish to see the works in the courtyard gardens, charmingly landscaped collections of plants and art. These are in the center of the building complex. The majority are representative of the earlier schools of contemporary sculpture, including two Henry Moore works, two Henri Laurens and an Aristide Maillol. There is also a Seymour Lipton work and a David Wynne *Girl with a Dolphin* in the center of a fountain. Of particular note are the wonderful heavy figures of Laurens, *Le Matin* and *Les Ondines,* which you reach by walking on stones through a watery environment that heightens your appreciation for the art so beautifully placed.

For those of you who enjoy nature as well as sculpture,

notice rare plantings, including some from Japan and China. A list of these trees is available at the Visitor Center; but we will also mention a stand of birch trees, an oak grove, a stand of witch hazels, lacebark pine from China, European hornbeam, black locusts, sweet gum, walnut, hemlock, cypress and dawn redwood. Among the wonderful flowering plantings are azaleas, rhododendrons and crabapples, so you might want to take this walk in April or May—at the height of the flowering shrub season. In any case, we think you'll find this combination of natural and artistic pleasures a rare treat.

INFORMATION

The Donald M. Kendall Sculpture Gardens at PepsiCo's headquarters are on Anderson Hill Road in Purchase, New York. The Sculpture Gardens are open free from 10:00 A.M. to dusk, seven days a week, year-round. Wheelchair accessible. Telephone: (914) 253-3000.

DIRECTIONS

From New York, take the Hutchinson River Parkway north to exit 28 (Lincoln Avenue). Note sign indicating SUNY/Purchase. After exit go left on Lincoln Avenue to its end. Turn right onto Anderson Hill Road; entrance is on the right.

Frank Lloyd Wright's "Usonia": A Planned Community

Pleasantville, New York

Usonia is no ordinary community. Nestled in rural Pleasantville, in the rolling hills of Westchester County, this unique enclave of some forty-eight modern houses set amid nearly one hundred acres of wooded land is distinctive in its architecture and philosophic raison d'être. The creative spirit behind Usonia was the great architect Frank Lloyd Wright, who designed its site plan, as well as three of its homes. To visit this community is to enter the fascinating world of this twentieth century master and to see firsthand a realization of his aesthetic ideals and philosophical concepts. A walk in this pretty area is also very pleasant, with hilly, wooded roads throughout.

The term "Usonia"—an acronym of United States of North America (with an added "i" for euphony)—was used by Wright to describe architecture for the "average U.S. citizen" (but also based on the writer Samuel Butler's "Utopia"). The term "Usonian house" applies not only to the specific houses in Usonia but to a type of house Wright designed in the 1930s and 1940s; it was meant for the average middle-income American. Intended to be simple in construction and proportion and, therefore, affordable, it was nonetheless anything but "average." Rooted in Wright's radical concept of organic unity, a Usonian house was totally linked to its environment. It was to be "a natural performance, one that is integral to site, to environment, to the life of the inhabitant. Into this new integrity, once there," wrote Wright, "those who live in it will take root and grow." Houses were made of natural materials—usually wood and stone—with large expanses of glass to relate the outdoors with the indoors; structures were low, with cantilevered rooflines, so they would blend in better with their natural surroundings.

In 1944 a group of Wright's admirers, seeking affordable housing in a cooperative setup in the country, retained Wright to design Usonia. The main instigator of the project was David Henken, a mechanical engineer who had seen an exhibit of Wright's, a project called Broadacre City, at the Museum of Modern Art. He had been so impressed that he then went to study with Wright for two years at his headquarters in Taliesin, Wisconsin. The idealistic Henken envisioned a Utopian community where responsibility and costs would be shared, ownership of property would be communal, and where everyone would live in harmony. (This utopian ideal has a long history in the United States, particularly in the nineteenth century, but Usonia was unusual for its time—the 1940s and 1950s—when individual rather than communal ownership was a goal of the "American dream.") He organized a nucleus of twelve families, all enthusiastic about the idea of cooperative living in the country. They pooled their financial resources—at first, $10 a week from each family for the cooperative. They found the ideal piece of land in Pleasantville for a mere $23,000. Wright—who had only agreed to building five of the proposed fifty-five houses plus the community buildings—began drawing up the site plans for Usonia. In the end, he built only three houses (in the late

1940s and early 1950s): the Serlin, Reisley, and Friedman houses, all of which can still be seen. Other architects with similar aesthetic ideas were engaged to design the remaining houses: Ulrich Franzen, Kaneji Domoto, Aaron Resnick, Ted Bower, and David Henken himself.

Wright designed circular, rather than traditional, rectangular, site plans. In this way there would be common land between each one-acre circle and the land would flow freely without the arbitrary divisions usually imposed in a traditional subdivision. There were to be no backyards or frontyards, and the houses were sited so that they would blend into the surrounding landscape, rather than disturbing the natural beauty of the area. The shapes of the houses were odd and irregular (the Friedman house is circular) to accommodate their surroundings. Even though there was a common theme that united the houses in Usonia and they were to be built in groups and not individually, each was designed to be distinctive.

By the early 1950s, practical problems plagued the cooperative. More money was needed to finance additional houses (a total of fourteen houses were built cooperatively), but banks were unwilling to grant mortgages to such a nontraditional group. There were also the inevitable problems concerning materials, schedules, and prices (the homes ended up costing more money than anticipated). Tensions and disagreements arose within the community. By 1955 individual owners—rather than the cooperative—had taken possession of their own homes and only the forty or so acres of recreational land were left for cooperative control. A similar fate engulfed most of the other cooperative communities that preceded this one (indicating perhaps that human nature may be more idealistic in the abstract).

Today the cooperative continues to maintain the roads, water system, and tennis court, and there is still a very strong feeling of community (very few of the original owners have moved away or sold their homes). The original utopian dream may have faded, but its legacy lives on, as you will see on your walk through Usonia. Though you will find only three houses Frank Lloyd Wright designed himself, all forty-seven structures adhere to Wrightian architectural ideas and each is interesting in its variations on the Wrightian plan.

This is a moderately hilly walk through lovely rock and tree-filled terrain, which would be enjoyable even without the added interest of the architecture. The site chosen for Usonia has a natural beauty all its own, like many Hudson Valley areas, and it has remained totally unspoiled.

Leave your car just off Bear Ridge Road at the intersection with Usonia Road. If you would like to know more about the origins and specific architectural details of what you will see before taking this artwalk, we suggest you write or call Roland Reisley before going. The directions that follow will, however, enable you to spot the major houses and sites.

As you begin your walk heading up Usonia Road you will see a modernish white house in what Wrightians somewhat satirically call the "international style" on a hill to your right. (It is not a FLW house.) But as you continue along Usonia Road, you will overlook to your left several contemporary homes below the road level. These are Usonia tract homes, though not of specific Wright design. If they interest you enough for you to want a closer look, take Tulip Tree Road, the first left you will come to, and walk down before returning to Usonia Road.

Continue along Usonia Road, where it overlooks a lovely valley and turn left on Orchard Brook Drive. Very soon you will spot a distinctive house wonderfully set on a hilly overlook. It is unmistakably by Frank Lloyd Wright. The master's touch is evident in the round portion of the structure and its distinctive interaction with the natural beauty surrounding the building. This is the Friedman house, one of three original designs for the site. Mr. Friedman was a toymaker, and Wright decided to design an appropriately playful house for him. (He later called it "House for a Toymaker.") You can take a detour here to see it from another angle if you wish, by walking along the road to its end.

The Friedman house is in the vein of Wright's prairie-style houses, characterized by horizontal wood siding, deep eaves, and a great deal of stone and glass. But it is particularly innovative in its use of round forms. The structure is designed on a plan of two intersecting circles, on which building cylinders rise and are capped by hat-shaped roofs. The view is unobscured by solid walls; the generous use of glass brings sky and forest to view throughout the house. Even the low stone wall surrounding the house is part of the design, creating a level for the cylinders to sit on. Wright described the Friedman house himself: "There will probably never be another Friedman house nor any closely resembling it. It is of the hill not on it, and I believe the Friedmans are loving it more and more."

If you continue along this road, bearing somewhat to the right, at the very end you will find the second Wright house of Usonia, the Serlin house. This one is less easily seen from the road, though you can view it from beyond the driveway without intruding on the privacy of its owners. The Serlin house is even more clearly based on the prairie house design, being low and horizontal. It too is set on a knoll with a wonderful view of surrounding hillsides and forest. Its rectangular forms, divided by areas of glass and horizontal wood siding, deep eaves, and the acute angles associated with Wright's designs make it a quite typical example.

Retrace your steps back to Usonia Road, passing some less spectacular, but nonetheless interesting, Usonia houses. Back on Usonia Road you will soon come to Wright's Way, a right hand turn. At a short distance on this little road is David Henken's own complex of houses and studios. The Henken family still uses this intricate compound of buildings. Though Henken designed this group, it seems thoroughly Wrightian. One of Henken's children, who grew up in one of these houses in Usonia, recalled the tremendous amount of glass and light: "In winter, I used to lie on the warm floor and look outside to the birds in the sun . . . the light coming in, with all the different angles in the house, was always shifting." It seemed to be the perfect setting for a creative family compound.

You will pass several other Usonia houses before coming to Bayberry Road. Turn right onto this road to make a loop passing by several interesting houses. Soon you will come back to Usonia Road near its end. Here you should turn left, reversing your direction on the main road. On your right almost at once you will find what is often considered Wright's best Usonia house.

The Reisley house was built for its current occupant, who now finds himself somewhat of the local historian on the subject of Usonia. Mr. Reisley will tell you many interesting details about the founding and building of the community if you make an appointment with him. (Please do not just "stop by," however, for people who live in original homes still deserve their privacy!)

The Reisley house, designed by Wright and partially completed by 1953, was quintessentially Wrightian both inside and out. It should be viewed from several angles. Your first look at it will be from below as the road rises up the hill. Keep walking up the road to get another, quite different, impression. It too was designed as a prairie house, with low, rectangular forms and acute angles. It has the combination of fieldstone and wood that Wright preferred, and small cabinlike windows along the horizontal wing.

Like the other Wright homes, the Reisley house was designed to blend in with nature; for example, its low stone walls look like a natural rocky ledge. Among its features are a balcony overlooking the wooded terrain and a twenty-foot cantilevered living room. Some of the furniture was designed by Wright and was built-in. The interior contains a dramatic, irregularly shaped central room with lovely views of the hillside, and small angled bedrooms. A stone fireplace, also set at an angle, is the centerpiece of the living room.

As you go back toward your car, you will have a new sight of each contemporary house along the way. You also will spot the amusing metal sculpture garden of one artist along Usonia Road (just to the left after the Reisley house).

If you have found the Usonia idea intriguing and want more information on it, you might be interested to look up a 1958 exhibition catalog devoted to Usonia from the Hudson River Museum in Yonkers, New York (telephone: 914-963-4550). In addition, some of Wright's ideas for utopian communities were expressed in his exhibition for Broadacre City (a 1940 exhibition at the Museum of Modern Art); the catalog can be found in a good library.

INFORMATION

This route is on a paved road and is wheelchair accessible. To contact Roland Reisley, telephone (914) 769-2926.

DIRECTIONS

From New York City, take the Henry Hudson Parkway to the Saw Mill River Parkway to Hawthorne Circle. Take Route 141 North to Pleasantville. Turn right on Lake Street and right again on Bear Ridge Road, to intersection with Usonia Road.

13

Georgian Court College: A Neoclassical Delight

Lakewood, New Jersey

The very name "Georgian Court" suggested to us an 18th century setting in an English countryside, with a stately home, arched bridges over gently flowing water, white marble statues, and formal gardens. We were both astonished and delighted to find exactly such a place hidden away in Ocean County, New Jersey, a treasure for explorers and art lovers, as well as more than 1000 college students.

Georgian Court College is a beautifully situated campus that was once a very large private estate. It is enclosed by walls along a wide shady street, and when you enter its palatial gates you come directly upon a setting of such felicitous proportions and so many neoclassical sculptures that you find it hard to equate it with the general run of the American college campus. Instead of modern kinetic sculpture, you find a fountain statue of Apollo; instead of hard trodden paths from dorm to dorm, you find stone walkways through formal sunken flower beds and a Japanese tea house.

The college (an undergraduate Catholic women's institution, with coed night and graduate divisions) was once the home of George Jay Gould, the financier and railroad magnate. Its one hundred and seventy-five acres were purchased in 1896. Gould hired a noted architect, Bruce Price, to design the home in the outskirts of the "winter resort" of Lakewood. The mansion itself (now a college building) was constructed of gray stucco with white terra-cotta brick, marble, and wood. The interior of the original building is elegantly paneled and maintained. There is an indoor marble pool; and outdoors, where the grounds were designed to match the Georgian era architecture, there is a lagoon and a sunken garden and a magnificent promenade.

Gould's son, Kingdon Gould, sold the estate to the Sisters of Mercy in 1924, and though they transformed it into an educational institution, happily they left its distinctive character in tact. In 1985 Georgian Court College was declared a National Historic Landmark.

The estate is situated along the banks of a good sized lake called Lake Carasaljo in the pines area of south central New Jersey. As you enter the gates you will come first to the Italian or Classical gardens, which harmonize so nicely with the architecture of the original mansion. This elliptical formal garden consists of some sixteen flower beds bordered by boxwood. The flower beds are meticulously maintained. A Japanese garden, made in 1925, includes a tea house, wooden bridges, and shrubbery.

As you leave the flower gardens and walk on into the center of the campus, you will find the rolling green lawns dotted with pathways and classical marble sculptures. The most notable sculpture is the Apollo Fountain designed by John Massey Rhind, a sculptor of public monuments and statues. Its horses plunge dramatically from the serene water, its white marble Apollo heroically in command.

A flight of wide marble steps takes you down to the lake edge and connects the original sunken garden and a lagoon, but the view can be seen from above. A promenade in the opposite direction (leading to classroom and library buildings) is flanked on either side by classical sculptures.

INFORMATION

Georgian Court College is open to visitors who wish to walk around the campus. The address is 900 Lakewood Avenue, Lakewood, N.J. 08701. The campus is mostly flat and wheelchair accessible. For information call (908) 364-2200.

DIRECTIONS

From New York, take the New Jersey Turnpike to the Garden State Parkway, Exit 91. Bear right after the toll plaza and proceed through the first intersection (Burnt Tavern Road) to the next traffic light, at County Line Road, which you take for approximately 5 miles to Route 9. Turn left on Route 9 South and continue to Ninth Street. Turn right on Ninth Street and proceed through the Forest Avenue intersection to Lakewood Avenue. The entrance to the college is to your right.

14

A Romantic Riverside Walk

Nyack, New York

This is a beautiful, romantic riverside walk in which the Hudson River is so close you can actually put your feet in at any moment. The winding path is a one-way trail along the riverbank, but you will find it interesting and varied even when you retrace your steps. The red sandstone, shale and traprock cliffs of the Palisades at Hook Mountain border the trail on one side, while the gently lapping river flanks the other.

The trail is totally flat, with occasional picnic tables and lookout rocks. You can go 1.7 miles to the end or do any part of it, remembering that you have to walk back.

This is an all-season walk, although it can be cold and blustery in winter. However, many enjoy it particularly then, when large ice floes dot the river and bang up against the shoreline. Even on the hottest summer days the walk is pleasant, breezy, and partly shaded. In late spring you will find a wonderful variety of wildflowers. As might be expected, Sundays are more crowded, although we have never found it unpleasantly so. The rest of the time it is a mostly quiet, solitary walk.

We recommend this outing for anyone, including families with children. But remember that young children must be kept from the temptation of climbing too high up on the

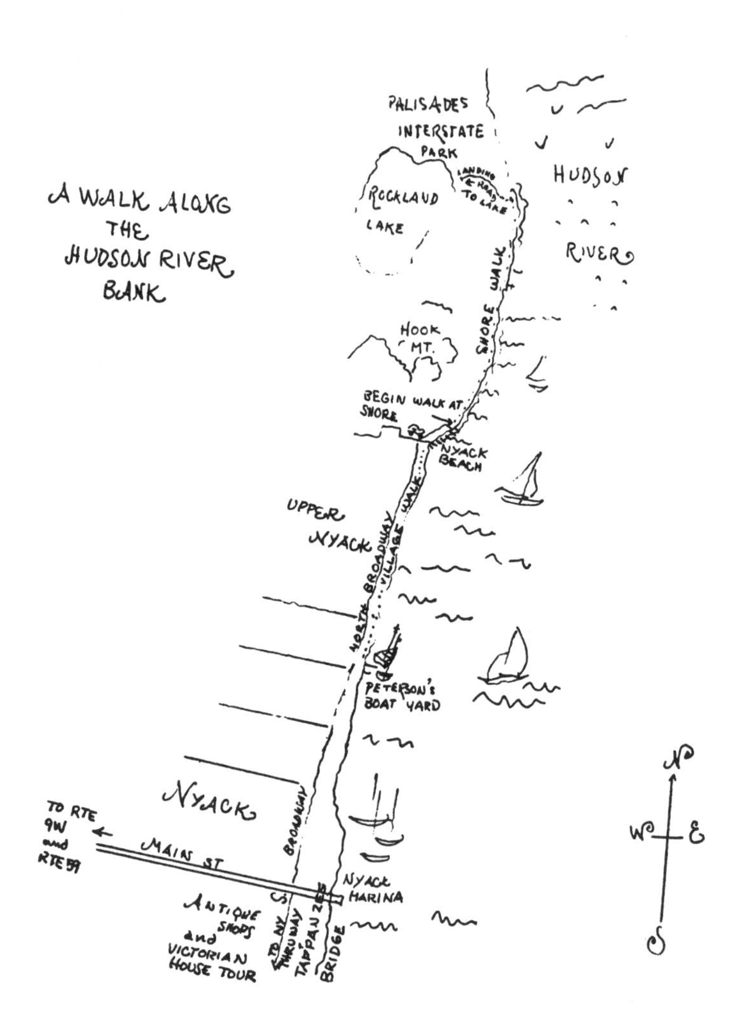

rocky outcroppings. Strollers of all ages will love this cool, breezy trail.

Bring a picnic, as there are no concessions along the way. Any good, comfortable shoes will do, since you will find the path soft and easy on the feet. This is a fine walk for picture taking or sketching, with the ever-changing river at your side. Some people ride bikes on the trail, while others bring their dogs. Leave your car in the parking area by the river and head north on the narrow cinder trail before you.

If you're walking in late spring you'll enjoy the array of wildflowers and plants that flank the path on both sides: wild geraniums, roses, daisies, honeysuckle, wild grape, tall grasses that bend with gentle breezes. There are dramatic clusters of rocks along the mountainside forming majestic cliffs that dominate the landscape. These steep cliffs were quarried in the late nineteenth century to provide rock for growing New York City. Some thirty-two quarries cut rock from sites along here; it was then barged down the river to the city.

At every bend you will come to great river views. Take your binoculars and observe life on the river. On Sundays sailboat races are often held, and occasionally you'll spot a Hudson River schooner sailing by. Across the water you can see the historic sites of Washington Irving lore: Philipse Manor and Sleepy Hollow Manor and the village of Ossining, with its formidable Sing Sing prison. To the north you might see Croton, if it's a clear day, and the Croton Point Park jutting out onto the river. On the river itself, in addition to the passing boats, you might spot a variety of ducks or geese swimming by lazily.

Occasionally you'll cross a hidden path going up the hill to the left into Hook Mountain State Park, but we suggest you stay on the main trail, which is the most scenic.

After about one mile you will reach an especially attractive lookout point. If you've taken your dog (they are allowed here as long as they are leashed), this is a good place to let it wade into the Hudson! You can stop and rest at one of the picnic tables here and take in the view.

If you continue north you will come to Landing Road, a fairly steep paved road to the left, which will take you into Rockland Lake State Park. This marks the end of our walk, although you may wish to continue.

If you do go on, after about five minutes' walk up the road

you will see a smaller paved path to the right, which goes back down to the river, then north, paralleling the river for several more miles to the town of Haverstraw. On your return you will have the Tappan Zee Bridge before you, as a focus for your walk.

If you're not tired after the walk you might wish to explore further. From the parking area walk back up the paved road and reenter the park going uphill this time, to the wonderful plateau of Hook Mountain. There are playing fields, more picnic tables, and views galore. This is a great spot for children!

If you are still in the mood for more activity, drive to the village of Nyack, now quite an antique center. Most of the antique (and craft) shops are located on South Broadway from Depew Avenue to Main Street, although there are some on Main Street as well. Sundays are fairly busy, when tourists and collectors arrive en masse. Those who prefer ambling at a more leisurely pace would enjoy strolling through during the week; most of the shops are open Tuesdays through Sundays.

In addition, we suggest you at least catch a glimpse of the following:

1. In Upper Nyack, on your way south from the park, stop and look at the Old Stone Church, the oldest in Rockland County, dating from 1813. The church is located on North Broadway near Birchwood.

2. Petersen's Boatyard on Van Houten Street, off North Broadway, has been functioning since 1898. Although there are no boat rentals, it's fun to browse around.

3. Edward Hopper House, 82 North Broadway, is the boyhood home of the artist Edward Hopper. Built in 1858, it is now a small art gallery that shows works by Rockland County artists. The Hopper House provides short walking tour maps of some of the local places Hopper knew and painted.

Nyack has some special events that might interest you:

There are two annual street fairs, in May and September, featuring arts, crafts, and antiques, when many dealers set up shop on the streets in town. Call 914-358-5234 for information.

INFORMATION

Nyack Beach State Park is open daily from 8:00 A.M. *until dusk. There is a small parking fee in season. Although the path is not paved, it is accessible to wheelchairs.*

DIRECTIONS

From Manhattan's west side: West Side Highway, George Washington Bridge, Palisades Interstate Parkway, exit 4, north on Route 9W. From exit 4 you will go about nine miles north to get to Nyack Beach State Park. (After about 5.5 miles you come to a blinker light. Bear right, take Broadway and keep going straight, past the village of Nyack. You will run right into the park. Take the road to the right, down the hill, to the parking area.)

From Manhattan's east side: FDR Drive, Harlem River Drive, George Washington Bridge, and then follow the same directions as above.

15

The Palatial Grounds of Longwood Gardens

Kennett Square, Pennsylvania

The Longwood Gardens hardly need an introduction. Among the finest of their kind in the east, they are a major tourist attraction year-round. And with good reason. The meticulously tended flower beds, topiaries, sunken gardens, grand allées, water gardens, and conservatories are a delight to all, young and not so young alike. There are some 350 acres to explore, including an arboretum with ancient trees, a Victorian grotto, meadows of wildflowers, and forest lands. Walking through these beautiful grounds is a joyful experience; it is also easy and pleasant, as the terrain is flat and many paths paved. You can join a guided tour (Longwood is well organized in that respect) or pick up a walking guide at the visitors' area and launch out on your own adventure. You will find you can easily lose the crowds in this extensive area, as you wander through the many individual gardens (eighteen in all), walk around the idyllic lake (complete with Grecian temple), or enjoy a picnic in the pastoral parkland.

Visitors are particularly drawn to the wonderful conservatories and the water gardens with their exceptional spectacles. Indeed, water gardens were the passion of Pierre S. Du Pont, founder of Longwood and dedicated gardener in his own right. He had admired the exquisite water gardens in

Europe and tried to duplicate them here, adding touches of whimsy and elements of surprise that continue to fascinate today's visitors.

A collection of fountains, canals, pools, basins, and moats graces the landscape, and the soft and appealing sounds of moving water are often heard. The Main Fountain Garden—a huge 5-acre sunken area with rows of carefully trimmed maples surrounding the waterways—features special water events: water pours from the mouths of carved mythical creatures during five-minute intervals; 200 jets shoot off water in fan-like shapes and arcs three times daily during the summer; and on summer evenings extravaganzas of fountains, lights, and music are held, much in the tradition of the French "son et lumière" shows (some say these are even more spectacular). At the Open Air Theatre a curtain of water completes the decor and water displays occur regularly during and after dance performances.

Unlike the water gardens, the conservatories—seven in all—can be enjoyed at any time during the year, especially in winter, when their bright blossoms are most appreciated. The glass gardens include an Orangerie (a charming 1920s crystal palace), the East Conservatory (where children can amuse themselves wandering in an ivy maze designed especially for them), and five interconnecting conservatories. You'll find desert plants, palms, greenhouses of orchids, a collection of insect-eating plants, bunches of brilliant flowers hanging from baskets, topiary forms in large tubs, artistically arranged vegetable displays, and neat rows of nectarine trees.

In spring you can enjoy the Flower Garden Walk with masses of lilacs, roses, tulips, irises, and peonies bordering each side of the brick path; the Rose Arbor; the Hillside Garden with its azaleas and bluebells; and the peony and wistaria gardens. The Topiary Garden, with sixty yews trimmed in curious geometric shapes, is always a popular spot.

The main house on the estate—surprisingly modest considering it belonged to one of the country's wealthiest families—can also be visited. There are many special events at Longwood Gardens, in addition to the water displays described above, and you might wish to coordinate your visit accordingly: a November indoor and outdoor Chrysanthemum Festival; Christmas displays of poinsettias; indoor spring flower shows; band concerts, organ and choral recitals, and ballet performances; special programs for children and classes in horticulture and gardening for adults. There are even firework displays on special occasions during the summer.

The Longwood Gardens are indeed a year-round celebration of nature's joys.

INFORMATION

The Gardens are open daily, from 9 A.M. to 6 P.M. (November–March from 9 A.M. to 5 P.M.) There is an entrance fee. Conservatories and shops are open daily, 10–5 (later, when there are special events). The Du Pont House is open daily, April–December from 11 to 3. Admission is free. Facilities include a restaurant, cafeteria, and gift shop. Gardens, conservatories, and shops are all wheelchair accessible. For information on special events call (215) 388-6741.

DIRECTIONS

From New York City take the Lincoln Tunnel to New Jersey Turnpike south to exit 2, Route 322 west, across Commodore Barry Bridge into Pennsylvania. Continue on Route 322 west (it becomes I-95) for about a mile, following signs for West Chester. At intersection with Route 1 turn left and take Route 1 south for about 8 miles. Follow the signs for the Longwood Gardens.

16

The Thomas Cole House and Frederick Church's "Olana"

Catskill and Hudson, New York

The Hudson River painters—the American Romantics who glorified nature on canvas in the mid-nineteenth century—drew much of their inspiration from the Hudson Valley, where many of them lived and worked. Thomas Cole, known as the "Father" of this school of painting, and Frederick Edwin Church, his illustrious pupil, both lived here. This outing takes you to their homes, which are located on opposite sides of the river (see directions at the end of the chapter), just minutes—but light-years—apart.

The Cole House, an unpretentious, white clapboard structure, was the residence of Thomas Cole. Olana, the grand Persian-style villa dramatically perched atop a hill overlooking the Hudson, was the home of Frederick Church. The Cole House is as modestly understated as Olana is wildly extravagant: While the former is an ordinary early nineteenth century American farmhouse, the latter is the result of an imagination fueled by the aesthetic fantasies of exotic lands. The contrast between them could not be greater—in architectural style and ambience—yet each provided an inspiring setting for the creation of important works of art.

Thomas Cole moved to his farmhouse in the village of Catskill, located 115 miles north of New York City on the west bank of the river, in 1836. His desire was to live and paint in this glorious spot with its views of the river and the Catskills. (Today these views have been partially obscured by overgrown trees on the property.) As he grandly stated, "The Hudson for nature magnificence is unsurpassed . . . The lofty Catskills stand afar—the green hills gently rising from the flood, recede like steps by which we may ascend to a great temple, whose pillars are those everlasting hills, and whose dome is the boundless vault of heaven." While living here he painted some of his great Catskill landscapes (see chapter 5). His pictures are odes to nature, with their unusual sensitivity to its nuances and intensity, its lights and shadows. He was able to nurture his mystical need to commune with nature in these environs, without having to go far afield. "To walk with nature as a poet is the necessary condition of a perfect artist," he wrote. As his concerns were for spiritual and aesthetic—rather than material—values, it is not surprising that he was not a commercially successful artist. His home reflects his simple life-style and tastes.

The Cole House remains much like it was, except for the overgrown vegetation on its three-and-a-half-acre property. The small foundation that now operates it has tried to keep the place as Cole knew it, without giving it the new gloss of a facelift. (You might think that it could use a coat of paint here and there!) Because most of Cole's furniture and personal belongings were sold some years ago, the interior of the house is now quite bare and you will find few personal mementos. But a visit to this quiet and refreshingly uncommercial spot will give you a sense of who Cole was as an artist and person. You will most likely be able to enjoy the place by yourself, as there are few visitors and no guided tours.

To reach Olana you travel only three miles but enter another world. A spacious 250-acre park surrounds the sixteen-room villa, which is often crowded with tourists. The approach to the house is itself on a grand scale, with a network of roads winding up the hill. The house is at the top, with commanding views that Frederick Church captured so beautifully in several of his paintings.

Church was first introduced to the Catskills—"Nature's great Academy of landscape art"—in 1844, when he came to study with Thomas Cole, but it was not until fourteen years later that he decided to live here. By then he had become an international celebrity. He had traveled throughout the Americas, from Ecuador to Labrador, as well as in Europe and Asia, to experience firsthand natural wilderness at its most elemental. He had created showpiece landscapes that literally galvanized the public, who flocked to see them. His *Niagara* was hung by itself; it was so popular it could only be viewed by ticketholders. His *Heart of the Andes,* a massive 5½' × 10' canvas that became one of the most celebrated American paintings of the century, was actually preached about in pulpits, where ministers extolled Nature's glories. It would have been unlikely for Church, with his flamboyant style, to have gone off to paint in a quiet spot, as Cole did.

After marrying in 1860 he bought a 126-acre farm south of the town of Hudson, intending, in fact, to live a quiet, rural family life. But with time he inevitably thought in grander terms and acquired more land. Seeing himself as landscape designer in addition to painter, he began to convert the property into a Romantic landscape garden; he created reflecting ponds, planted thousands of trees and many flower gardens, and constructed carriage roads that were carefully placed to enhance a sequence of views. He also decided to build a larger house. What began as plans for a French château changed dramatically, when Church returned from a trip to the Middle East, enthralled with Moorish architecture. The architect Calvin Vaux (the co-designer of Central Park with Frederick Law Olmsted) was engaged to design something exotic, but it was Church himself who ultimately created Olana ("our place on high," in Arabic).

Church made sketch after sketch, followed by elaborate drawings, much as if he were conceiving a large painting; and he became involved in every detail of the house—from the colors, shapes, and sizes of the rooms to the placement of windows to frame river views, from the interior decor to the colorful stencils inside and out. He further enhanced the surrounding gardens to complement the house, adding lookout points where views could be captured. Olana became much more than a place to live; it became a work of art to Church.

You can appreciate Olana as Church's personal creation when you visit the house and surrounding grounds. A forty-five-minute conducted tour leads you through the house, now a museum, where you enter the private world of the artist. In contrast to the Cole House, Olana is filled with artifacts, objects from years of travel, vintage furniture, works of art, and memorabilia that vividly recall Church's rich and fulfilling cultural and family life. But perhaps the best way to understand Church's art is to wander through the vast property, which you can do on your own, and enjoy the naturalistic gardens and breathtaking views that so inspired him. Before you begin your walk pick up a guide to the landscape, available at the ticket office. A map indicates points of interest, including the site of the studio where Church first painted. (He later designed and built a new studio wing onto the main house.) It was probably from this spot that he captured the views immortalized in such landscapes as *The Catskills from Olana*.

INFORMATION

The grounds of Olana are open daily all year, from 8:30 A.M. to sunset. You will find joggers, walkers, and picnickers enjoying the surroundings. The museum is open by guided tour only, from April 15–October 31, Wednesday–Saturday, 10:00 A.M.–5:00 P.M. and Sunday from noon to 5:00 P.M. (Note: The last tour begins at 4:00 P.M.) Tours are limited to twelve people, so reservations are recommended, particularly in view of the fact that Olana is a popular place with some 25,000 visitors to the house annually. There is a moderate entrance fee. Mostly wheelchair accessible. Telephone: (518) 828-0135.

The Cole House is open Wednesday–Saturday, 11:00 A.M.–4:00 P.M. and Sunday 1:00–5:00 P.M. during the summer season. There is no admission fee. The house is not wheelchair accessible. Telephone: (518) 943-6533.

DIRECTIONS

To get to the Cole House: From New York City take the New York Thruway to Exit 21 in Catskill, then Route 23 east to the traffic light at Route 385. Turn right and go about fifty feet to the entrance of the Cole House on the left.

To get to Olana from the Cole House: Take Route 385 to Route 23, turn right and cross the Rip Van Winkle Bridge (where you should note the extraordinary views). Turn right on Route 9G for one mile, following the signs, and wind your way up the hill to Olana.

17

A Towpath Walk Along the Delaware Canal

From New Hope, Pennsylvania

The level towpath that runs alongside this picturesque canal is an ideal walking route. Originally built to accommodate the mules that pulled barges along the canal—as they still do today—the towpath is narrow and overhung with trees; it is a scenic delight as it winds along the waterway. It is flat for walking, and the only impediments to a solitary walk are occasional joggers and bikers and other walkers, in addition to the mules who still ply the canal drawing barges now filled with sightseers.

If you start at its beginning, the canal walk can cover almost 60 miles, and as a matter of fact, hardy walkers do just that, either taking their camping gear along, or sleeping at inns along the route. Our chosen walk is quite a bit shorter, though you can lengthen it at will, particularly if you have a car parked at the other end. It is especially nice on a spring day, when the willow trees along the way are at their lightest green, and when the canal seems bright and clean.

Keep in mind as you walk that you are never very far from civilization, and you can turn off the towpath now and again for refreshment at a nearby village. We preferred, however, to stay on the path, taking a picnic lunch with us.

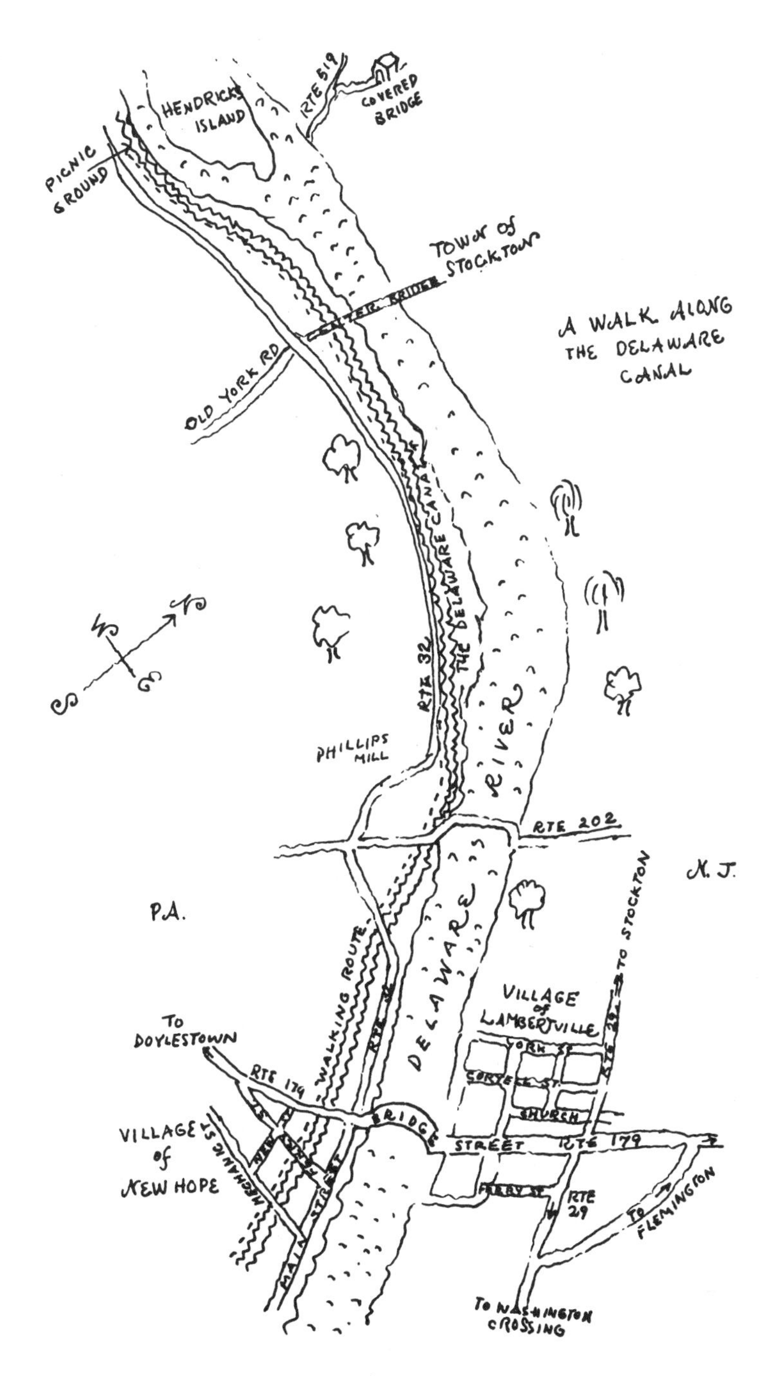
HENDRICKS ISLAND
RTE 519
COVERED BRIDGE
PICNIC GROUND
TOWN of STOCKTON
A WALK ALONG THE DELAWARE CANAL
OLD YORK RD
THE DELAWARE CANAL
RTE 32
N
W
E
S
PHILLIPS MILL
RIVER
RTE 202
N.J.
P.A.
TO STOCKTON
DELAWARE
WALKING ROUTE
VILLAGE of LAMBERTVILLE
TO DOYLESTOWN
RTE 179
YORK ST
CORYELL ST.
CHURCH
BRIDGE
STREET
RTE 179
VILLAGE of NEW HOPE
MECHANIC ST
MAIN STREET
FERRY ST
RTE 29
TO FLEMINGTON
TO WASHINGTON CROSSING

As we mentioned above, spring is the ideal time for this walk, although fall is also very pleasant. Summer finds New Hope such a tourist mecca that we hesitate to add more people to the crush. The towpath is always open, so even winter walkers can use it if they enjoy the crisp waterside winds.

There are no restrictions on visitors to the towpath, or on what they take along. You can bring your dog, a picnic, and whatever else you would like to have. We suggest strong walking shoes and birding binoculars.

This canal, which is steeped in history, covers an area of Pennsylvania that is beautiful both in natural scenery and in architecture. The old stone houses for which Pennsylvania is well known sit smack along the towpath, surrounded by giant sycamores, tulip poplars, locusts, oaks, and overhanging weeping willows. Rhododendrons and hill laurel abound—another reason to go in spring. Fishermen enjoy the canal for catfish, perch, and carp, in addition to small-mouthed black bass that have traditionally been caught here. Shad, once a flourishing crop, are just beginning to make a comeback.

Birders will be well rewarded on this walk. Among the waterfowl seen at any time of year are mallard and black ducks and night herons; summertime brings egrets and ospreys. Other birds to look for are owls, downy woodpeckers, Carolina wrens, ruffed grouse, marsh hawks, ring-necked pheasants, and turkey vultures, in addition to the more common robins, cardinals, and goldfinches. In summer you might see—or at least hear—whippoorwills. The profusion of birds along the canal is due to its proximity to the Delaware River, which serves as a guide to migratory birds—in particular to Canada geese; they can sometimes be heard honking in early mornings as they wing their way along.

Begin this section of the canal walk at New Hope, a jumble of antique shops, historic houses, and tourist spots in a scenic location along the Delaware River. The canal goes right through New Hope and the towpath is easily reached just east of Merchant Street. (You might want to see lock no. 8 in New Hope before setting out.) Walk out of town along the path heading west. You will first pass the New Hope and Ivyland Railroad, which runs a steam train excursion on weekends in the tourist season. As you leave the bustle of New Hope, you will come to Rabbit Run Bridge, and then in about 1.5 miles to Phillips Mill, built as a grist mill in 1756. Once a thriving art colony, Phillips Mill is now a small community surrounding the converted mill—a nice place to take a breather. About .5 mile farther you can spot the remains of two old kilns where the lime industry once flourished; here lime was mixed to make mortar and crop fertilizer. About three miles from New Hope you'll come to Center Bridge, once known as Readings Ferry (named for Colonel John Reading who established the first Delaware River ferry in 1711). At that time a major route from New York to Philadelphia crossed here. When you reach Center Bridge, cross over to see Stockton in New Jersey, known for its fine stone houses. There is an inn on each side of the water here. (About a mile farther on the New Jersey side you'll find route 519, which leads to a fine covered bridge.)

The sight-seeing barge stops at a picnic area surrounded by rhododendron, where there are picnic tables, grills, and a comfort station. In the center of the canal is Hendricks Island, which virtually fills up the canal. You will now have walked just under five miles. If you continue (assuming you have a car waiting for you), you can walk on to Lumberville, where there is another lock and nice scenery (about two miles along from your picnic site). From there go to Point Pleasant (two more miles), where you'll find the remains of a river bridge and a sandy swimming beach on the Delaware. The walk continues for many miles, eventually ending at Easton, Pa., where the Lehigh River meets the Delaware.

After (or before) explore New Hope and its across-the-river neighbor, Lambertville. The ferry between the two villages was built in 1726 and was known as Coryell's Ferry. You can still visit the site; other historic reminders of the importance of this area in the Revolutionary War are all around, from Washington's Crossing about three miles east, to several historic houses in New Hope. The boats used by General Washington in the crossing of the Delaware were hidden on a small island in the Delaware near Lambertville, and the hill called Goat Mountain, just to the south of the village, was where Washington was taken to view the island and make sure the boats could not be seen. The Parry Barn Museum in New Hope (Main Street) is a fine 18th-century mansion built at the end of the Revolution and now operated by the New Hope Historical Society.

Reminders of the busy days of canal traffic also still exist: in New Hope you can take the canal-barge ride mentioned above. You can also take a river sight-seeing trip in a small boat from Coryell's ferry landing in Lambertville. For a train ride on one of the few remaining coal-burning trains around, try the excursion line mentioned above; it goes puffing along for 14 miles through scenic Bucks County, beginning in New Hope.

Those interested in historic houses and architecture might enjoy one of the various walking tours of New Hope with its many shops (pick up the guide at the Parry Barn Museum or any shop, or just walk along Ferry, Main, and Bridge streets).

Also worth a visit is the well-known Bucks County Playhouse, which presents professional summer stock in a 250-year-old gristmill on the water. For information call 215-862-2041. A play can be a nice way to end a day of canal walking and exploring a bustling village.

INFORMATION

If you prefer to take a barge trip contact the New Hope Barge Company at (215) 862-2842 for a one-hour excursion—a charming and leisurely outing, accompanied on occasion by a folksinger or tale-teller.

The walk is unpaved but flat and may not be fully wheelchair accessible.

DIRECTIONS

New Jersey Turnpike to exit 9. Take Route 1 south toward Trenton. Pick up Route 95 (295) south after Princeton (at Bakersville) and take the highway to the exit at Yardley, Pa. Take Route 32 West to New Hope.

18

Chesterwood: The Home and Studio of Daniel Chester French

Stockbridge, Massachusetts

The lovely region of western Massachusetts known as "The Berkshires" is endowed with charming vistas, mountains, rivers, lakes, and little New England villages. The area has long attracted seekers of unspoiled natural beauty, including many artists and writers.

Daniel Chester French, the famed neoclassical sculptor of monumental works, came to establish a summer home and studio in the shadow of Monument Mountain near Stockbridge, Massachusetts. When you visit Chesterwood, his remarkable country estate, you will come away feeling that he could not have chosen a more idyllic spot. He was an artist who really knew how to live.

French became the nation's leading classical sculptor in the early decades of this century. After studying the Beaux-Arts style in Paris in the late 1880s, he returned to America to establish his own studio. He began his illustrious career making allegorical figures that represented the lofty civic and patriotic aims of the nation.

Along with Augustus Saint-Gaudens, he produced many of the most important neoclassical statues at major sites all over the country. Among his colossal allegorical female figures were sculptures titled *The Republic* (a commission of the World's Columbia Exposition in Chicago in 1893), and the *Four Continents* (at the New York Custom House, now the home of the National Museum of American Indians).

Later works combined portraiture with personification. Giant figures that were both lifelike and monumental brought him increasing fame and public commissions, among them his most notable work, *The Lincoln Memorial* in Washington, D.C. (You will see the various working versions of this statue at Chesterwood.) French's ability to create heroic, allegorical figures in a naturalistic style was well-suited to the taste of the nation, and even after the advent of modernism, he continued to receive honors and awards.

At the height of his career, internationally known and able to live in grand style, French decided to create a perfect working and living environment for himself and his family in the country (although he continued to maintain a winter studio in New York). He and his wife first saw the rustic farm that was to become Chesterwood while on a horse-drawn carriage trip through the Housatonic River Valley in 1896.

Beautifully situated on a rural road, the 150-acre property—now a museum operated by the National Trust for Historic Preservation—would become the Frenches' summer home for the next thirty-three years. It was at Chesterwood—amid the enchantment of romantic gardens, lawns, and woodlands—that French was inspired to create many of his most important works, including the *Lincoln Memorial,* the *Minute Man* for Concord, Massachusetts, and the *Alma Mater* for Columbia University.

Chesterwood itself became a lifelong project for the sculptor. Carefully he fashioned the estate to provide an ideal ambience for his creative needs, as well as for the many brilliant social gatherings he was fond of hosting for his prominent neighbors and friends. (Edith Wharton came regularly from her nearby estate.) The main house and studio, overlooking majestic Monument Mountain, were designed by his architect friend Henry Bacon; but it was French himself who laid out the garden and woodland walks.

To him gardens were like sculptures: a basic design had to be drawn up in order for them to work as art. He planned a central courtyard, an Italianate garden with a graceful fountain, and English flower gardens. Beyond the formal areas he arranged a network of paths leading into and through the hemlock forest, where the walker could enjoy peaceful views. He enjoyed creating aesthetic effects that influenced the quality of daily life. For example, he built a berm (an artificial little hill) abutting the road leading to the house; in that way one would not see the wheels of approaching carriages, which would appear to be "floating" by.

French spent a great deal of time in his garden, from which he derived much of his inspiration. He regularly studied the effects of light and shadow on sculptures that were destined to be out of doors. He found an ingenious solution to moving these massive works from his studio to the outside. He would put these pieces onto a revolving modeling table set on a short railroad track and roll them out into the sunlight, where he could test them in the natural light. You can still see this unusual contraption when you visit the studio.

French and his wife lived and thrived at Chesterwood with their daughter, Margaret Cresson French, also a sculptor. In 1969 the property was donated to the National Trust and converted into the museum you see today.

When you arrive at Chesterwood you are struck by the beauty of the site: with spectacular mountain views on all sides it is little wonder that French and his family wanted to be here. The house and landscaping are tasteful and harmonious in every sense; there is nothing pretentious or ostentatious about this estate. As the artist once remarked, "I live here six months of the year—in heaven. The other six months I live, well, in New York." A possibly discordant note (and a recent one) is an ongoing modern sculpture exhibit, which is on view on a rotating basis throughout the grounds (including the woods). The pieces we saw had nothing to do with French, his style, or his era and were in striking contrast to the gracious nineteenth century setting.

In order to visit the house and studio you must take an organized tour—about forty-five minutes of fairly detailed information (more than you might want to hear), including a great deal about the social life of the French family and mores of the time. However, you are free to roam the grounds and woods at will, and can do so at no cost. After you have purchased your tickets for the house and studio you will probably be directed to the barn to begin the tour. This rustic building, originally part of the working farm that French purchased, has been remodeled into an exhibition gallery. You can wander about and look at the vintage photographs and works by Margaret French Cresson, Augustus Saint-Gaudens, and others.

Aside from the gardens, the studio visit is by far the most satisfying part of the tour. The beautifully designed twenty-two-foot high structure provided the perfect airy and spacious working environment. It is kept much as it was during French's time, with materials, notebooks, tools, and sketches on view. You'll see plaster cast models and preliminary sculptures of some of his most important works, notably his seated Lincoln (of which there are several versions) and his graceful Andromeda. You'll also see the massive thirty-foot double doors that were constructed to accommodate French's many large works; they were built when French first made his impressive equestrian statue of George Washington, now located in the Place d'Iena in Paris. Off to the side of the studio is a cozy room with couch, piano, and corner fireplace where French entertained. Apparently he enjoyed having friends around even when he worked. In back of the studio is a wide veranda (which he called a "piazza") with wisteria vines and fine views and the rail tracks on which his massive sculptures rolled away.

The thirty-room colonial revival house (built in 1900) is nearby. Its gracious rooms, wide hallways, and appealing surroundings are what you would expect from a man of French's refined tastes. Surrounding the house are the charming gardens that French carefully planned and so enjoyed. Take a stroll in them and beyond, on the pine-laden woodsy paths in the forest. In the vicinity are two other inviting sites: Hancock Shaker Village (at the junction of Routes 20 and 41 in Pittsfield; telephone: (413) 443-0188). Once a Shaker community at its peak in the 1830s, this collection of simple houses and community buildings—including a round stone barn—is an architectural pleasure. You can also watch crafts being made in traditional Shaker style.

The Mount (at the junction of Routes 7 and 7A—Plunkett Street, Lenox; telephone: (413) 637-1899. The Mount was Edith Wharton's Gilded Age mansion and summer "retreat." Now a certified landmark with tours, resident theater company, etc., it is quite a tourist attraction. But if you enjoy gardens and interior decoration of the period, or are familiar with her influential books *The Decoration of Houses* and *Italian Villas and Their Gardens,* it's a "must see" spot, for she based the design of the imposing house and extensive gardens on her own precepts.

INFORMATION

Chesterwood is open May–October, from 10:00 A.M.-5:00 P.M. It is recommended you phone first to check on the next sched-

ule; most of this site is wheelchair accessible. Telephone: (413) 298-3579. There is an inexpensive entrance fee.

DIRECTIONS

Chesterwood is about two miles west of Stockbridge. From Boston take Route 90 (the Massachusetts Turnpike), to exit B3 to Route 22; go about one mile to 102 to Stockbridge. Take Route 102 west to junction with Route 183. Turn left onto 183 for one mile to a fork in the road. Turn right onto a blacktop road, travel a few yards, and turn left. Continue 1/2 mile to Chesterwood.

19

Wethersfield: The Delights of Trompe L'Oeil

Amenia, New York

There are many ways in which gardens can be artistic—or appear to be art themselves. Topiary gardens are like parks of living sculpture, while sculpture parks are themselves gardens of art. At Wethersfield, a country estate near Amenia, New York, you'll find gardens that are at once repositories for sculpture and themselves a kind of spatial work of art. As you walk through the landscaped grounds of Wethersfield you'll have a sense of trompe l'oeil—that French description of art that plays spatial tricks on the unsuspecting (but delighted) viewer.

Wethersfield's gardens are so artful that the eye can be deceived by the long allées and decorative gates, and the geometric shapes of pruned bushes and trees that form the setting for its marble statuary. The gardens within gardens, the sense of perspective, the carefully placed statuary, reminded us of the surreal gardens of René Magritte's paintings, where a hat may appear over a hedge in a dreamlike green garden of distant proportions and uncertain boundaries.

The gardens are the high point of the visit to this gentleman's country estate (and working farm). There are also tours of a spanking carriage barn with elegant vehicles of the past, all shined up and ready to go (the owner participated in carriage driving competitions), and a house tour through the large interior, which, despite some real art treasures, is not terribly interesting.

If you want to see everything, you must call for an appointment. On your (prearranged) arrival you can decide which parts of the estate are of most interest, but you will surely want to explore the gardens (which can be visited separately), even if you skip the carriage barn or the house tour.

Wethersfield has just opened formally to the public. It was the home of Chauncey Stillman, an investor and philanthropist, who purchased it in 1937. The estate now consists of one thousand four hundred acres. The setting of the house and gardens is magnificent, overlooking a vast panorama of fields and mountains—the Catskills to the west and the Berkshires to the north. The gardens cover more than ten acres of the estate and provide a marvelous place to walk. There are also woodland paths that you can enjoy at your leisure.

The Georgian-type mansion, built in 1940, is in a traditional colonial style. It houses Stillman's collection of antiques, paintings, furniture, and decorative objects. Elaborate and somewhat overwhelming frescoes by the present-day Italian artist Pietro Annigoni cover a number of walls in a sort of neo-Baroque fashion. There are several paintings of serious interest, including a wonderful *Boy with a Dog* by Toulouse-Lautrec, two Mary Cassatts, an Ingres, a Sargent, and a Degas, as well as many lesser works.

There is a great mix of styles and attitudes in these interiors, ranging from the owner's rather chummy den with its duck-embroidered pillows, to a room that functioned as a Catholic shrine to the Pope, with a Murillo painting over the mantel. The most startling room is the south wing which Stillman called the "Gloriette," an addition to the house in

1973, which can only be described as eccentric in style and taste. The guide will describe it all.

And now to the gardens. Leave yourself plenty of time to see them, and even to walk through the woods to the Palladian arches at the edge of the field. Pick up a map at the upper parking lot, where you leave your car. You'll find the brochures in a basket between two stone lions.

The gardens, which you will enter here, are generally neoclassical and French in style. They are simultaneously grand and intimate. You might even see occasional peacocks strolling through them. Each garden is separated from the next with hedges or wrought iron gates. Though there are formal flower beds, it is the geometric design of borders and flagstone paths, reflecting pools, and green walls of hedges that create the special ambience of this place. There are cones, balls, columns, and boulder-shaped topiary designs, as well as gargoyles and cherubs, temples, animal sculptures and classical figures everywhere, nestling into the greenery and demarcating each individual area.

You'll find a lily pond with sculptured turtles, deer sculptures by John Flannagan, two Pans by an Englishman named Peter Watts, two nymphs and a Hercules of limestone, some charming recumbent sheep, a naiad by the Swedish sculptor Carl Milles gracing a fountain, and a stone stairway leading to a "Belvedere" with a stunning view of the landscape.

A Polish artist named Joseph Stachura made many of Wethersfield's sculptures, including the Madonna and other religious works around the grounds. They are representational marble carvings that are graciously placed here and there in shrinelike settings.

All of the sculpture is traditional—this is not a venue for the latest in abstract works. Instead, it is a period setting with a strikingly "modern" sense of space. Like an outdoor gallery, the gardens are a form of three-dimensional art, ornamented with sculpture; the emphasis of the landscape design has surely been on form.

But this is not to say that there are not charming flower beds and wonderful trees. There are, in fact, a rose garden, perennial gardens, a cutting garden, and many other distinctive sections. (An army of gardeners works year-round.)

INFORMATION

Wethersfield House, Gardens and Carriage House are open Wednesday, Friday and Saturday, June 1 through September 30. To visit the house or carriage house or garden you must make an advance reservation. The gardens are open noon to 5:00 P.M. There is a moderate entrance fee. Wheelchair accessible throughout. Telephone: (914) 373-8037.

DIRECTIONS

Wethersfield is located in northern Dutchess County, New York. From the Taconic Parkway, take Route 44 north of Millbrook, then take Country Road 86 (Bangall-Amenia Road) and turn right onto Pugsley Hill Road. Follow signs about 1 1/3 miles to the entrance on the left.

20

Battery Park City: A Contemporary Urban Park

New York City, New York

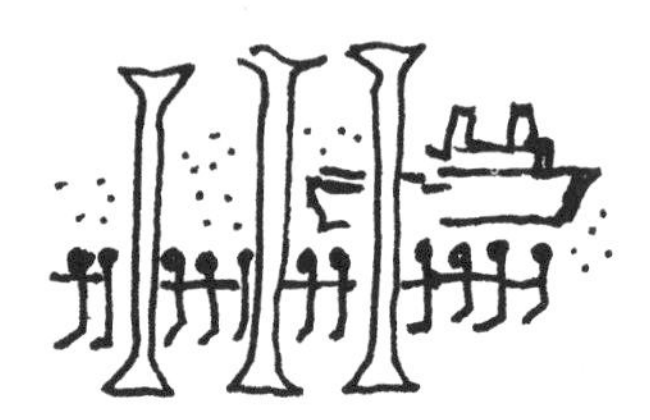

A visit to the new Battery Park City to see some of New York's most interesting outdoor art sights is well worth taking. Battery Park City is a planned community of high-rise apartments and parks that face the Hudson River. The designing of artworks to enhance the site has been a part of the project from the beginning, and works by Mary Miss, Ned Smyth, R. M. Fischer, Richard Artschwager, and Scott Burton (among others) are very much in evidence. The Battery Park City Fine Arts Program has become a sort of test laboratory for the combining of architecture, city planning and art at a spectacular site; it is fascinating to view this contemporary version of an ancient idea.

At the north end of Battery Park City, you'll find the stunning Winter Garden, a large, interesting, airy indoor space with shops, restaurants, and a particularly attractive open area. While there are occasional art exhibits among the palm trees of this neo-Edwardian atrium with vaulted glass roof, it is mostly used for concerts and other public functions. But on the balcony level there are regular art shows; a recent exhibit was called "Masks of Mexico." Outdoors there is a plaza which is in itself an environmental work of art. Designed by Cesar Pelli, M. Paul Friedberg, Siah Armajani, and Scott Burton, this grand space includes granite benches and chairs (by Burton) that are an integral part of the design.

Across the way you will see what appears to be an Egyptian temple set before you. *The Upper Room* (1984–87), a large work by Ned Smyth, is one of the more intriguing outdoor sculpture complexes to have been placed in the city's open spaces in years. Made of a pinkish combination of stone, mosaic, cut glass, and cast concrete, its forms are definitely ancient, somewhat Egyptian, a touch classical Roman, with here and there a Renaissance arch. The spacing and design of the series of columns, seating areas (there are even inlaid chess boards), a kind of altar, an arcade, and the varied textures of the stone are fanciful and appealing. The view of the promenade along the river and the far shore adds to the tranquillity of the spot. Smyth tried to create what he called a "space of respect"; he also wanted his work to relate well to the architectural complex of the new community being constructed around it. Gestures of postmodernism in the buildings are echoed in his arches and details, while the pinkish color of the sculpture picks up the warm brick tones of the architecture. It's a nice place to interrupt your walk for a few moments and to imagine yourself surrounded by ancient (but crisply new) ruins.

Walk along the shoreline to the northern edge of Battery Park City for a must-see stop at the brand new Hudson River Park. These 8.2 greenacres include a playing meadow and children's playground complete with carousel, child-size bridges, climbing nets, slides, games, swings, and animal sculptures. But of particular interest is "The Real World," an enclosed paved terrace featuring some fifty whimsical bronze sculptures by Tom Otterness. Conceived as a playground to stimulate the curiosity of children, it is an unusual collection of odd objects and creatures—animal, human, imaginary, real, giant, and lilliputian—in the most imaginative and unlikely combinations. Children and adults alike will delight in these sometimes surreal, always clever vignettes: a cat dressed in a bowler hat plays chess at a picnic table; Humpty Dumpty fiddles away, while a creature looking like a vacuum cleaner/dinosaur is about to attack; a dog carefully observes a cat stalking a bird about to catch a worm; a frog atop a lamppost looks down on the proceedings, while a fierce-looking dog is tightly chained to a water fountain. Footprint and penny motifs (in apparent acknowledgment of nearby Wall Street) can be found throughout, in the most unexpected spots. Overscaled bronze pennies and child-size footprints are interspersed in a winding stone path and an island made entirely of pennies is surrounded by a moat. Children will enjoy discovering and identifying these and the other items that are sometimes cleverly disguised by Otterness's intricate designs.

Battery Park City has other sites to visit as well. Walk south along the windy landscaped promenade, one of the city's nicer amenities. En route you'll find Rector Park, an unusually charming spot with wrought-iron fence and elegant plantings. Don't miss Rector Gate, an airy steel construction that faces the park. Created by R. M. Fischer in the late 1980s, it consists of various circular shapes—globes, open spheres, cones, and a lacy cupola—in an imaginative arrangement. Just beyond, at the end of Thames Street, is "Sitting/Stance," Richard Artschwager's rather obscure park furniture sculpture garden.

All of the art at Battery Park City was commissioned by the city and was chosen expressly to enhance the new site. One of the most important and successful of these commissions is environmental artist Mary Miss's design for the esplanade at its south end. Her proposal for the shoreline included a lookout, pilings that rise and fall with the river tide, wooden wisteria-covered archways, boardwalks lighted with blue lanterns, and Japanese-style rock gardens. The architect, Stanton Eckstut, and a landscape architect, Susan Child, helped execute her design. While the site-art is surely a form of gentrification of the natural shoreline (you can see what the banks originally looked like, just over the fence at the edge), it is a major attempt to balance the sophisticated urban setting on the shore with the Hudson's rather wild and somber coastline. From the top of the curving steel staircase, you can enjoy an extraordinary view of the shapes and patterns of Mary Miss's design, as well as of the city, the river and New Jersey.

From here you can wend you way back to the crossover at the World Trade Center.

INFORMATION

These sites are all wheelchair accessible and are flat and paved for easy walking.

DIRECTIONS

Subway to World Trade Center, or park at lot near World Trade Center. From Liberty cross the Westway highway (either by overhead walkway or by street level at the traffic light) to reach the far side of the World Trade Center complex. Turn south and walk on South End Avenue to Albany Street, where you turn once again west, toward the Hudson River.

21

Outdoor Art in the Philadelphia Region

Montgomery County, Pennsylvania

The outskirts of Philadelphia are a particularly lovely area for walking and for enjoying art. The rolling terrain, luxuriant foliage, and great old fieldstone estates make an incomparable setting for sculpture. A number of these old mansions and their surrounding grounds have become colleges, museums, private schools and arboretums.

The Abingdon Art Center is in Jenkintown, northwest of Philadelphia. The township of Abingdon has recently made Alverthorpe Manor—an old and gloriously landscaped estate—available to serve as an art center for the surrounding communities. Its first exhibition opened in 1990 with large outdoor sculptures and a small indoor gallery. The center plans to change exhibitions yearly, to hold three month site-specific exhibitions, multifaceted art programs (some 250 courses in art are offered), and a variety of gallery events.

Of major interest to us were the magnificent space for open air sculpture and an ongoing environmental art project in a woodsy area. The sculpture garden lies behind the charming stone central building. A veranda behind the house looks out on a vast greensward, set with modern sculptures.

This is a good walk if you wish to view each artwork close up. The ancient trees and beautiful lawns make this a particularly nice outing for springtime. Be sure to pick up a brochure describing each piece of sculpture at the central desk before you set out.

When we were there the year-long exhibition included works by Alice Aycock, Melvin Edwards, Roy Wilson, George Greenamyer, Mary Ann Unger, and Jude Tallichet. All of these artists are well-known in the world of contemporary sculpture, with site-specific pieces in many other public locations, and numerous solo and museum exhibitions.

But Abingdon also offers juried sculpture shows for what are known as "emerging" sculptors from the Delaware Valley area. A recent juried show (judged by Alice Aycock) featured stipends to artists and teams of artists to construct new works on the sculpture garden grounds. Another exhibition, called "Ancient Sources: Contemporary Forms," explored ancient and archetypal imagery in modern sculpture. No matter what show is on exhibit when you visit, you will find a wide variety of contemporary styles and ideas awaiting you in the luxuriously landscaped gardens.

In addition, you will want to veer to the side of the major sculpture garden to visit the environmental site of one of the more unusual art setups we have encountered. There we found a sculptor and landscape artist named Winifred Lutz working away on a wooded area of the estate. Deep among the fallen trees, roots, overgrown bushes and piles of leaves, she is attempting to "reevoke a sense of woodland history by reclaiming the land." The artist intends to restore one or two acres, making "a register of wood that has fallen" and several large installations involving the fallen tree trunk and paths that follow the footsteps of deer. While this description may make her objectives sound somewhat obscure, you will find the site work itself intriguing, for she has stacked up wood by sizes in giant piles, filled in the vee of a fallen tree with wood, and laid out a series of pathways leading to a stone folly she has found, that is perhaps a hundred years old. If you are lucky she will be there working with axe and saw and will tell you how her plan is materializing and how she visualizes the finished result. This may be a rare opportunity to watch an environmental artist at work. (If you visit when she is not there—or in the unlikely possibility that this massive undertaking is permanently finished—the curator at the center will no doubt explain it to you.)

While you are in this immediate area, you might want to detour to the nearby Tyler School of Art, the fine arts division of Temple University. The campus is open to visitors, who will enjoy the exuberant young talent displayed all across the grounds and in a nice gallery within the main building. We saw some avant-garde works, including large outdoor sculptures—one called *Metabolism and Mortality* involved a kiln and six burners sending flames through the portholes of a vast globe stuck with sticks—and an indoor exhibition relating to shoes and costume constructions. If the latest student art is to your taste, stop by this campus—you'll enjoy a walk here.

Also not far away is the campus of Beaver College, whose central building is a sight to behold. One of those grandiose concoctions of the late nineteenth century, Grey Towers was the home of William Welsh Harrison, a sugar refining magnate. The well-known Philadelphia architect Horace Trumbauer designed this medieval style castle, with crenellated turrets, forty rooms, a grand staircase and—of particular interest to us—a large number of hand-carved medieval-style gargoyles. You don't have to go to Europe to see gargoyles! The carved stone heads of gods and demons with grimacing faces ornament Grey Towers in many easily seen spots. You'll find them all around the porticoed entranceway. These will be "finds" that children will particularly enjoy.

You can also walk into the main hall to see the grandeur of the building, including fine decorated ceilings (nymphs, garlands, and clouds) in a mirrored ballroom, commissioned tapestries, and gold and cream carved, decorated walls that rival those in the finest palaces abroad. (The decorator's bill in 1898 came to $50,000 for painting and tapestries alone.) Other artistic oddities include Pompeiian-style murals in what was Mr. Harrison's smoking room, and a flat-vaulted ceiling in the Great Hall that is modeled after one at the château of Chambord in France.

In contrast with the grand and ancient style of Grey Towers there used to be a number of contemporary outdoor sculptures visible on the campus. But at our last visit they had been removed for a major construction project. You can inquire in Grey Towers as to their whereabouts.

Finally, make your way to Morris Arboretum of the University of Pennsylvania. Located well outside the city in a greenbelt, this is a lovely, hilly, Victorian-style park, filled with both flowers and sculpture. Though the plantings and pathways are quintessentially Victorian and some of the loveliest we have seen, the sculpture is anything but old-fashioned. In fact, you might consider most of it totally unrelated to its surroundings.

The Morris Arboretum is at the site of a great house called Compton, which once belonged to a prominent Quaker couple named John and Lydia Morris. Though the house is now gone, the 166 acres of landscaped grounds remain, and are kept in the most beautiful condition. This is a rather long and hilly walk if you want to see everything—and you should.

Originally designed by Charles Miller (an American of Anglophile tastes), the park is a marvel of charming paths, flowering shrubs, fountains and clustered garden areas. There is a Temple of Love on a Swan Pond. There are numerous great trees—including twelve redwoods bordering a stream—a grove of cedars, the most magnificent flowering cherry tree we have ever seen, and many rare trees from the Orient. (You can pick up material on the arboretum—including a map and information on what's blooming—when you enter.)

There are also many flower beds in the English style, as well as an indoor grotto with more than five hundred types of tropical ferns. The rock garden, azalea meadow, and holly slope are all worth seeing. In June don't miss the rose garden bordered by a wisteria allée. We could go on and on about the flowers and trees—but you will discover for yourself the natural beauties of Morris Arboretum. Be sure to plan your visit according to the season you most enjoy.

Now to the sculpture: The art works are somewhat dwarfed by the beauties of the landscape. The Butcher Sculpture Garden contains predominantly contemporary art of which there are about a dozen permanently installed sculptures.

Several Cotswold sheep made of two-dimensional Cor-Ten steel by Charles Layland are "grazing" at the base of Magnolia Slope. A kinetic steel sculpture by George Rickey called *Two Lines* moves in the wind. You'll see several constructivist pieces on the grounds including Israel Hadany's *Three Tubes,* Buki Schwartz' *Four Cut Stones,* and a painted metal sculpture, *Untitled,* by George Sugarman. Linda Cunningham is represented by a giant bronze and steel sculpture that evokes the garden idea; its name is *Germination.*

At the center of the sculpture garden is a group of modern works by Scott Sherk based upon classical Greek mythology (but without classical visual connotations). Robert Engman is represented with a rotating geometric sculpture called *After B.K.S. Iyengar* (a yoga master). Thomas Sternal has made two wood sculptures from felled trees from the Arboretum's own grounds; one is called *Table,* the other, *Altarpiece.*

The Morris collection also features several more traditional pieces, including a *Mercury at Rest* (a copy of an antique sculpture excavated at Herculaneum) and some portrait sculptures of the Morrises themselves. Children will enjoy the Lorraine Vail whimsical animal characters, including a five foot frog and a bull.

The sculpture is widely separated by glorious patches of nature, which may give some viewers a sense of the art as a secondary source of decoration (as in Edwardian times). In fact, this type of massive contemporary art does not readily lend itself to such cultivated surroundings—except for young Mercury seated on a stone. Nonetheless, you shouldn't miss the experience of kinetic sculpture amidst the blossoms.

INFORMATION

Abingdon Art Center is at 515 Meetinghouse Road in Jenkintown. Telephone: (215) 887-4882. There is no admission fee for the sculpture garden.

Tyler School of Art is at Beech and Penrose Aves. Elkins Park. Telephone: (215) 782-2700. The campus can be visited during daylight hours, year-round.

Beaver College's Grey Towers Castle is at Easton and Church Roads in Glenside. Telephone: (215) 572-2969.

The Morris Arboretum is at 100 Northwestern Avenue, Philadelphia; telephone: (215) 247-5777. It is open 10:00 A.M. to 4:00 P.M. daily; guided tours are available on Saturdays and Sundays at 2:00 P.M. There is an admission fee.

All of these sites are partially wheelchair accessible.

DIRECTIONS

All of the sites listed are north of Philadelphia. From Philadelphia take Route 611; from the Pennsylvania Turnpike, take exit 27 to Route 611. To reach the Abingdon Art Center in Jenkintown take Meeting House Road from 611. Tyler School of Art is in nearby Elkins Park; go south on Route 611, right at Cheltenham Avenue, take third right on Penrose Avenue. Beaver College is on Church Road which also intersects Route 611. To reach the Morris Arboretum take Stenton Avenue (which also intersects Route 611 a bit farther south) and head northwest (right). The Arboretum is between Stenton Avenue and Joshua Road on Northwestern Avenue.

22

The Noguchi Museum and Sculpture Garden and Socrates Sculpture Park: Exploring Queens' Left Bank

Long Island City, New York

Perhaps the most unlikely setting for a walk and truly memorable aesthetic experience is a visit to the bleak industrial area of Long Island City that lies just south of the Queens end of the 59th Street Bridge. Here, amid old warehouses and unidentifiable blocks of buildings, are two wonderful spots to visit—only a few blocks from one another. You will find yourself in this neighborhood very quickly after you exit from the Queensboro (59th Street) Bridge; you may be surprised to discover fine art in this decidedly commercial neighborhood.

Here, however, are two sculpture sites within a short distance of one another. Your first stop will be the Isamu Noguchi Museum and Sculpture Garden (32–37 Vernon Boulevard)—a veritable shrine devoted to the works of one of the twentieth century's most influential and best known sculptors. In a setting of careful calm and contemplation, including a sculpture garden filled with Noguchi's characteristic Japa-

THE ISAMU NOGUCHI GARDEN MUSEUM
and
SOCRATES SCULPTURE PARK

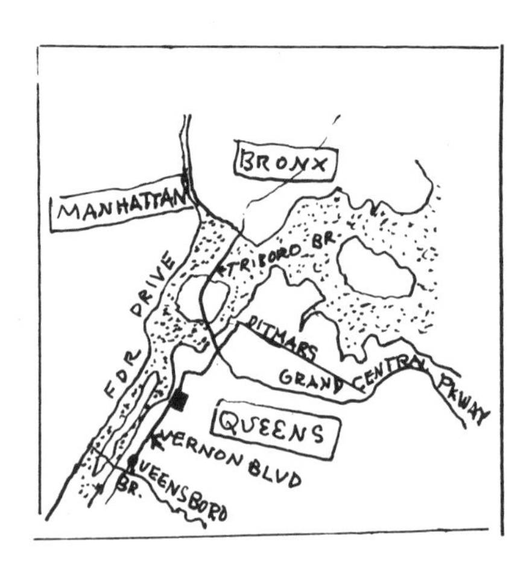

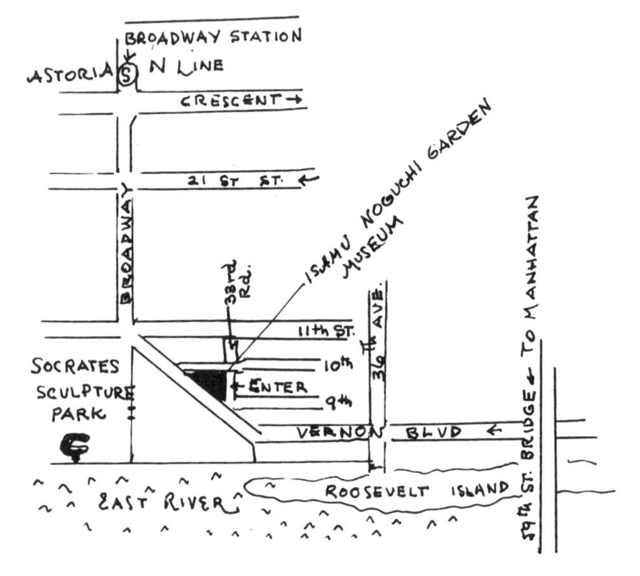

nese stone figurations, you can see the evolution of his art, from early figurative pieces to his most recent stone monoliths. The experience is an introspective one.

And in one of the curious juxtapositions of art sites in the many-faceted city, you'll find just blocks away, at the Socrates Sculpture Park, a collection of contemporary sculpture that is truly astounding in its freewheeling originality—some of it good, some fascinating, some quite awful. This most current collection sits on city-owned land on the banks of the East River. The seminal influence of such sculptors as Noguchi—the willingness to leave subject and representation behind in search of other truths—is evident everywhere, though there is nothing among these giant sculptures that vaguely reflects Noguchi's works themselves. Instead, you'll find changing exhibitions of vast and original works and—of particular interest—the artists themselves can often be seen working at their pieces in this unlikely, weedy field. You may wander at will through the towering constructions, waterside assemblages, and huge forms that are temporarily housed here.

The sculptures at the Noguchi Museum are mostly on permanent display, while those at Socrates Park change once or twice a year.

The Noguchi Museum and Sculpture Garden is about the best disguised art center we've discovered on our wanderings through the city. Set into blocks of old warehouses, it appears to be another nondescript, rectangular building, but on closer inspection you'll see the angles of a contemporary-style building nestling into its triangular city block. Noguchi wanted a home for his works that would be congenial to their style and to his concepts of art's relationship to its surroundings. "These are private sculptures," he said, "a dialogue between myself and the primary matter of the universe."

And what you will find at the museum are some 350 works that demonstrate the great Japanese sculptor's spiritual presence, as well as his evolving use of stone and other natural materials. The sculpture garden—walled off—brings traditional Asian design to the twentieth century. In these delicate stone works, trickling water fountains, abstract shapes, and patterns catch the light and do indeed give you the sensation of being very far away from both Manhattan and the twentieth century.

Yet Noguchi was, in fact, a quintessentially twentieth-century artist. His search was for abstract realities or what he called "the brilliance of matter" that will turn "stone into the music of the spheres." Everywhere—in the rough stone pillars, the delicate marble pieces, the rounded basalt mounds, the intricate black metal abstractions—you sense the sculptor's preoccupation with pure form and its relationship to the space around it. Under the artist's own direction, the museum has laid out works in a logical progression. In addition to the sculptures themselves, the museum includes many plans, drawings, and photographs of Noguchi's contributions in other places throughout the world. Among the fascinating examples are a photograph of a marble spiral for children ("to show how the idea of play relates to sculpture"), a dance set designed for Martha Graham ("the stage remained my main testing ground for many years"), and whole city plazas in detailed planning drawings—a particularly fascinating addition to the works themselves; they are a testament to his continuing interest in sculpture outside the studio. Among the oddities we enjoyed were paper lanterns and a musical weathervane designed by the artist. But most of all you will come away with a sense of the artist's serenity and spiritual presence that come through these often highly abstract, monolithic works. Although this is not art that is "easy" to understand for the layperson, it is nevertheless an experience that will change the way the most unreceptive observer of contemporary art looks at stone. You will have a new idea of how sculpture can both shape its surroundings and become a part of them.

The transposition to today's environmental sculpture is only a few blocks away. A short walk along Vernon Boulevard and the East River to 31st Street will take you to Socrates

Park, New York's largest sculpture park. At first you might think this is an unlikely spot for an important outdoor exhibition space, surrounded as it is with warehouses, industrial buildings, and random vacant lots. But the breathtaking views of Manhattan's skyline directly across the river and the waterfront site provide a dramatic setting for the large, avant-garde works on display. In these raw, unmanicured 4½ acres you will probably see the boldest, most original, and certainly most massive sculptures anywhere in the city—from huge steel abstractions piercing the sky, to rough-hewn constructions in fantastic configurations, original structures atop floating barges, and waterfront sculptures.

The brain child of sculptor Mark di Suvero, Socrates Park—which he named in honor of the philosopher who "had a lot to teach [him]" and of the Greek community in nearby Astoria—was created in the mid-1980s from an eyesore lot filled with heaps of rubble. The idea was to provide a space for large-scale outdoor sculptures where the originality, vision, and creativity of the works were to be considered rather than the fame of the artists. (Di Suvero was able to lease the property from the city for a nominal fee, and it has now become a city park.) From the beginning the community was encouraged to participate actively in the project, to make it an integral part of its daily life. Local residents, including teenagers, were hired to clean and tend the lot (tons of rubble had to be hauled away) and to be involved in running the park. As the sign at the entrance says, "Elevation 7 feet, population friendly." And so it is. Socrates Park is a real part of the community, used not only as an exhibition space for outside artists, but also accessible to local would-be artists who may be inspired to add their own unsolicited works to those on display. People come here to walk, to contemplate, to observe, to play. According to di Suvero, "you're *expected* to touch" the works, much to the delight of the neighborhood children, who can't resist the temptation to use the place occasionally as a wonderful, almost surreal playground. A visitor may be lucky enough to observe artists at work preparing for future shows. In fact, one of the park's programs—the Outdoor Studio Program—asks its artists to create their sculptures right here on site over a few weeks' time, when they are available to discuss their work with the public. On several of our visits we met informally with some of these sculptors and their assistants, all busy at work nailing down massive wood constructions, hauling huge steel parts, or preparing the soil for a future foundation. Chain saws, tractors, and other heavy equipment are often used to produce the massive works and prepare for shows, and neighborhood residents are invited to help in the construction and installation.

There are one or two exhibits annually, each lasting for several months at a time. The inaugural show, held on September 28, 1986, featured works by sixteen artists including Mark di Suvero, Vito Acconci, Rosemarie Castoro, Lauren Ewing, Mel Edwards, Richard Mock, and Sal Romano. Since then, shows entitled "Sculpture: Walk On/Sit Down/Go Through," "Artists Choose Artists," "Sculptors Working," and "Sculpture City" have been on view. Some of the works included have been Robert Stackhouse's *East River Bones* (1987), made from skeletons of sunken ships; Cristo Gianakos's *Styx* (1987), a huge double ramp with a platform (perfect for climbing); Jody Pinto's *Watchtower for Hallett's Cove* (1987), a tall wooden structure more likely to be found in the middle of a large field in a town in the Midwest; Malcolm Cochran's *Scrapyard Temple for Socrates* (1987), whimsical granite pillars around which colorful coffee tins with their labels have been attached in drapelike fashion; and Alison Saar's *Fanning the Fire* (1988), a totempole-like structure of wood, tin, and nails atop of which a stern-looking woman is holding a fan.

Mark di Suvero (whose waterfront studio is literally next door) often displays his works here.

At each of the park's exhibition openings you are likely to see performances by musicians, actors, or dancers in and around the sculptures.

INFORMATION

Note that the Noguchi Museum is open only on Wednesdays and Saturdays from 11 to 6 April–November. Telephone: (718) 204-7088. There is a small entrance fee. Socrates Park is open daily, 10 to sunset, seven days a week. Telephone: (718) 956-1819. Although Socrates Park may be rough going, since it is unpaved, the Noguchi Museum is wheelchair accessible.

DIRECTIONS

Subway: N train to Broadway. Walk several blocks (west) toward the Manhattan skyline to Vernon Boulevard.

Bus: From Manhattan there is a shuttle bus on Wednesdays and Saturdays only that leaves from midtown (from the Asia Society at Park Avenue and 70th Street) every hour on the half hour, from 11:30 to 3:30 and returns on the hour. For seasonal changes and fares, call (718) 204-7088.

Car: From the Queensboro Bridge, take the first right turn possible (Crescent Street) and another right on 43rd Avenue. Go to the end of 43rd Avenue and take another right on Vernon Boulevard. Turn right off Vernon Boulevard at 33rd Road. Entrance to the Noguchi Museum is on the left at 32–37 Vernon Boulevard. Easy parking on the street.

23

Smith College: Campus Pleasures of Nature and Art

Northampton, Massachusetts

Few college campuses take their gardens and botanical laboratories as seriously as Smith College. We recommend a stroll through this wonderfully inviting campus and its conservatories—as both students and visitors have been doing for over one hundred years. In fact, from its founding, Smith has been known for its spacious campus replete with greenhouses with tropical plants, outdoor gardens of all kinds, and intensive botanical courses.

In 1872, in its first handbook, the college listed botany and other physical sciences to which "particular attention will be paid." According to the college, serious study of botanical sciences began almost at once, a landscape firm and botanists were hired, and a building erected for the study of botany. "It is the first time in the history of the world," said the president in 1885, "that a building like this has been devoted to the study of science in a female college."

In the 1890s the landscape firm of Frederick Law Olmsted (of Central Park fame) laid out the huge campus, with instructions to make all of it serve as a botanical garden. Each building was to be surrounded with particular species of trees and plants. The first greenhouse was added in 1894 and soon after more greenhouses, laboratories, a "succulent house," a palm house and potting sheds. Smith College obviously intended its campus to be both beautiful and educational.

In 1894 a collection of exotic plants was begun—including dogwoods from China, weeping cherry trees from Japan, maples from Manchuria, and numerous other Asian specialties. More recent renovations have included updated conservatories and ever more trees and plantings as the campus expanded. Despite a harsh New England climate, the college has continually replanted and added to its tree collection. Its greenhouses have been put to extensive use, with cool and warm climates, a fern house, and areas for bedding flowers later to be planted throughout the campus.

In fact, a visit to this site may be happily scheduled during one of the two annual flower shows that feature the changing seasons. In spring, dozens of varieties of bulbs—tulips, hyacinths, narcissi, crocuses and other bulbs set with primroses and azaleas are featured. These more common American flowers are interspersed with exotic flowers from around the world. In fall, chrysanthemums—both familiar species and rare ones from China are the centerpiece. Each festival lasts for a week during which the campus welcomes thousands of visitors.

Your tour of the gardens should include: the Lyman Plant House (the major botanical laboratory site); the Rock Garden area (which includes exotic trees from Asia and a "Ben Franklin tree"); the Herbaceous Garden Area (where you'll find more than forty different species depending on the season, including everything from spiderwort to amaryllis, and cabbages to geraniums and sunflowers), and the Arboretum (with some 100 types of trees).

If you wish to see the delights of this campus in an orderly fashion, you should begin your walk at the Lyman Plant House and its entry at the Head House. (You will find it is open every day of the year and you may pick up a campus map there.) The staff even welcomes your questions.

Your tour of the facilities will take you to the Warm Temperate House (don't miss the grapefruit-size lemons and the pale violet water hyacinths). Next, the Stove House features goldfish swimming among such unexpected plants as rice, papyrus, and sugar cane. The Cold House comes next; it is filled with potted plants waiting for the spring, such as primroses and azaleas. Show House (between the Head House and the Cold Storage House) is where the flower shows are held. Beyond the Cold Storage House is a corridor of changing displays and camellias.

Beyond a series of laboratories you'll find the Temperate House, divided into four temperate geographic regions: Asia, Australia and New Zealand, Africa, and the Americas. Here your interest in exotic flora will be stimulated; specimens range from eucalyptus from New Zealand to American avocados.

From here you'll descend a ramp to the Palm House, a veritable jungle of rare palms and lush tropical plants, banyans and bamboo, cacao and cinchona. The Fern House—one of the oldest greenhouses on campus—is next; it too features plants from Asia as well as New England, including specimens from the East Indies and Tasmania. The Cold Temperate House will be next; you'll recognize it by the fragrant flowering olive tree.

On the south side of the Plant House is the Succulent House, specializing in Old World desert plants on your left, and New World deserts to your right. (The origins of these plants reads like an atlas index! Madagascar, Peru, the Sahara . . .)

Beyond these buildings you'll find the outdoor Rock Garden, where, in season, you'll find an exhaustively wide collection of dozens of plants of international origin—Swiss Edelweiss, African violets from the Pyrenees—we could go on and on. Here too is the famous Ben Franklin tree, now almost extinct except in cultivated gardens. The herbaceous garden that you'll come to next is a kind of outdoor laboratory that traces the evolutionary history of flowering plants. There is a pond here too—needless to say, it contains a large assortment of water plants.

You may now continue your walk across the campus to spot the many trees (all identified) and the beautiful layout of Olmsted's design. (We have not mentioned here the many artworks dotting the campus, but they are an added attraction to this outing. Information about them may be found at the college's Art Museum—also well worth a visit.)

There is a winding path—in springtime bordered by blooming trees and shrubs—and numerous trails that will take you to wonderful regions of mountain laurel in season, a giant redwood tree, and many other lovely places. In fact, you may find a stroll through these wilder regions of the campus your favorite part of this outing. But whatever your taste—for identifying the exotic, or merely for soaking up the perfumed and visual pleasures of the natural world—you'll find it here. But do be sure to pick up a map at the office to take with you before you set out!

INFORMATION

The campus of Smith College is open at all times to visitors. The campus buildings are all wheelchair accessible. The campus itself has a somewhat hilly, rolling terrain that is pleasant for walking but may be difficult for a wheelchair in some places. Call (413) 584-2700 for information.

DIRECTIONS

From New York, Hutchinson River Parkway to Merritt Parkway to Wilbur Cross (Route 15) to Route 91 North. Exit at Northampton and follow signs to Smith College.

24

A Reflective Lakeside Walk: Rockefeller State Park Preserve

Tarrytown, New York

This is a country walk surprisingly close to the city. The mixture of meadows, lake and wooded paths (with occasional horseback riders appearing on the bridle paths) gives the walker the feeling of being on an English country estate. The grounds and paths are well tended, but not overdone, the natural beauty of a Hudson Valley landscape unspoiled, the lake clean and rippling. The Preserve is indeed that—preserved for walking and enjoying the weather and feeding the ducks or observing nature. Despite its proximity to a bustling village and busy highways, once inside the preserve you'll find it hard to believe these 750 acres are not a hundred miles from civilization. The park was given by the Rockefeller family estate to the public just a few years ago, and apparently not many people know about it, for it is wonderfully uncrowded.

There are some 14 miles of carriage and walking paths, and the beautiful little Swan Lake covers 24 acres. There is a variety of terrains, including riverside lanes—the winding Pocantico River makes its way through the park—wetlands, woods, fields, and the path around the lake. Outdoor enthusiasts who use the preserve include birders, photographers, cross-country skiers, and artists, as well as horseback riders. The park asks its visitors not to disturb or collect anything. There is no picnicking, but you can take trail lunches to designated areas. Also forbidden are radios, unleashed pets, smoking, motorized vehicles, alcoholic beverages, and camping and swimming. These rules do not seem excessive, for the stillness and cleanliness of the grounds are a wonderful antidote to the bustle of life outside. It is an ideal place for reflection as well as companionable walking. The lakeside, in particular, is an oasis of quiet beauty, where you can watch the expanding ripples of water as a duck swims by.

This is an ideal walk for families, including elderly walkers or children. Most of the trails (all color marked) are not difficult and your walk can be as long as you wish to make it, for a good map (available at the entrance in a box on the side of the shed) will allow you to crisscross and combine

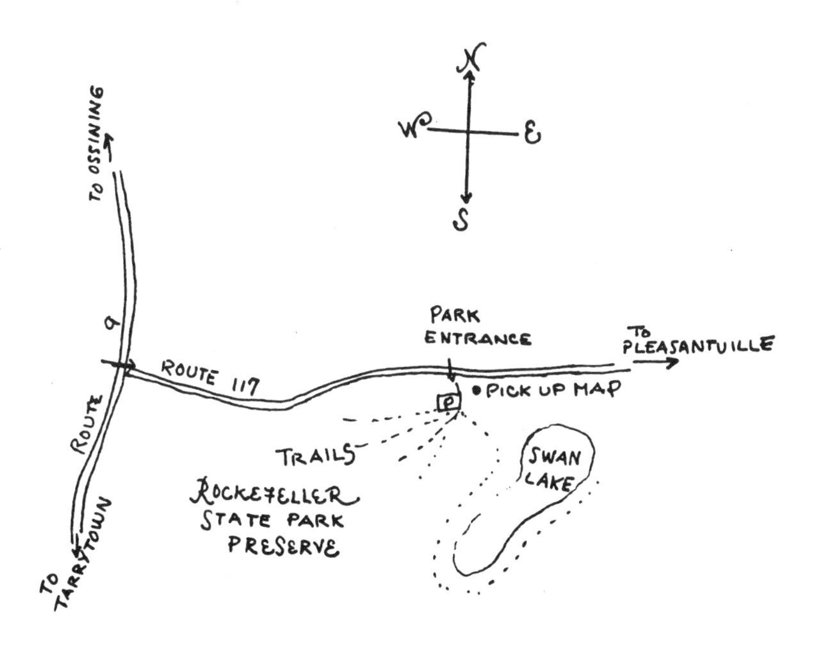

one trail with another. Take binoculars, some bread for the ducks if you wish, and perhaps a sketchbook or camera. The map at the shed lists the difficulty and length of each trail, so be sure to read it before you set out.

We recommend this walk in any season, including winter. Those walkers who enjoy a winter outing can't find a better one than this: parking is easy, the terrain is mostly level, and there are no snowmobiles or other noisy intrusions. Winter birds enjoy the lake and woods. In fall the foliage is glorious and its reflection in the still lake waters lovely to look at. Summer and spring are, of course, perfect times to visit, so this is indeed a year-round site for walkers.

Leave your car in the parking area and follow signs to Swan Lake.

INFORMATION

Although not paved, the trail around Swan Lake is mostly flat and wheelchair accessible.

DIRECTIONS

Take the Major Deegan north to the New York State Thruway to exit 9 to Route 9 north, through the villages of Tarrytown and North Tarrytown. Turn right on Route 117 and follow signs for the preserve. Entrance to the park is on the right.

25

Flushing Meadows: An Outdoor Gallery of Sculpture

Queens, New York

Perhaps you've noticed a massive metal unisphere alongside the Grand Central Parkway or Long Island Expressway, while driving to Long Island. Or perhaps you've passed some large, looming structures on your way to a sports event at Shea Stadium or the National Tennis Center. If you've never ventured into Flushing Meadows we invite you to discover an intriguing world—and not just the world represented by the giant unisphere. For the vast grounds (nearly 1,300 acres) at Flushing Meadows Park, once the scene of two World's Fairs—in 1939 and 1964—are filled with sculptures, pavilions, and odd abandoned structures from those events. Some of these relics are surprisingly good works, others merely forlorn curiosities, but you'll enjoy exploring them, as well as seeing more recent outdoor sculptures. And in a mall in the middle of the park you'll find the Queens Museum, with its worthwhile, albeit eclectic, exhibits and permanent collections—including its one-of-a-kind enormous geophysical panorama of New York City.

Bicyclists might also enjoy this outing, and bicycles can be rented for a modest fee at nearby Meadow Lake. The flat terrain throughout the grounds is ideal. On your outing you will enjoy exploring the vast park (now mostly a giant playground) with its expanses of lawns, rows of trees, lakes, and recreational facilities—a zoo, children's farm, game fields, and picnic areas. But you will especially be amused by the odd artworks interspersed here and there.

From the bike rental booth, take the path across the lawn toward the unisphere. Our first statue is a traditional one: a bronze *George Washington* (1) standing on a pedestal and looking appropriately presidential. It is by Donald De Lue, a well-known sculptor of works celebrating patriotic themes. (Another work by De Lue, *Rocket Thrower,* is next on our route.)

Nearby you'll find a small group (unfortunately only here temporarily) of distinctly untraditional sculptures bearing neither artists' names nor titles. These intriguing works include a chopping block, a giant propeller, an egg, and a carved tree within a circle of surrounding trees. (The site for these off-beat works is ideal; it seems a shame that more of the vast grounds are not used as temporary homes for contemporary works of this kind.)

You'll find *Rocket Thrower* (2), a more realistic statue, east of the unisphere, where it graced the Court of Nations at the 1964 World's Fair. Its creator, De Lue, was an American who specialized in the large symbolic figures that were so popular in the first half of this century. His *Rocket Thrower* is a giant male figure reaching dramatically into the sky to launch an arc-shaped object through a collection of stars, symbolizing space. It suggests reaching into the unknown.

Our next sculpture stands alone in a green field; it is an unusual and evocative memento of the past—the very distant past. Unlike people from other parts of the world, Americans are unused to spotting antiquities in their parklands. Here in Flushing Meadows you'll see the *Column of Jerash* (3), a gift from Jordan given to the World's Fair by King Hussein. Built originally by the Romans in 120 A.D., it was transported to Queens to ornament the Jordanian Pavilion, now long gone. It remains here in this unlikely spot—a lone, but very elegant column from a group of classical ruins known as "The Whispering Columns of Jerash" for the sound of the wind rustling among them.

Facing the unisphere (between Shea Stadium and the unisphere) is another striking sculpture: *Freedom of the Human Spirit* (4) by Marshall Fredericks. It is a green bronze statue of a man and woman reaching up to the sky. Three geese are poised to fly around them. Representational but symbolic in concept, Frederick's work joins the De Lue and de Rivera works (next on your route) in attempting to capture the optimism of the World's Fair and its theme of exploration and spiritual freedom.

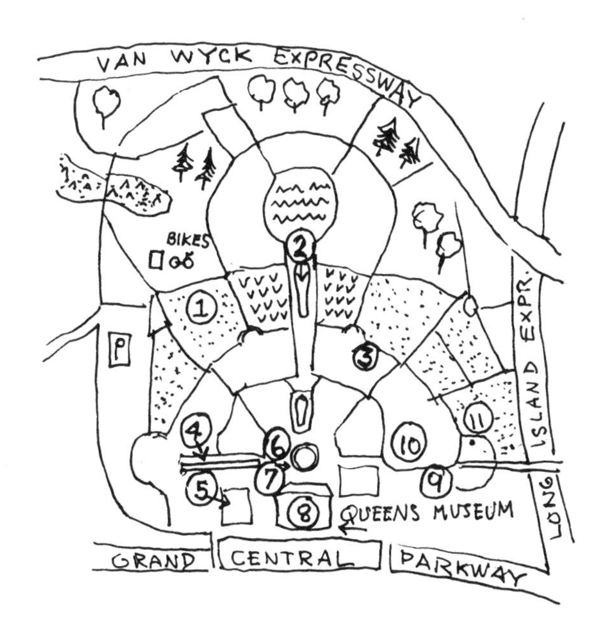

To the left of the museum is José de Rivera's *Free Form* (5), one of the most interesting sculptures in the park. A polished, curving metal construction, it resembles a giant boomerang. The nonfunctioning sculpture was meant to revolve, and the City hopes to repair its motor soon. It is made of granite and steel (de Rivera did much of his own forging and hammering). *Free Form* is well named; it soars into the sky like a free-flying bird. With their similar themes, #2, #4, and this de Rivera work make an excellent contrast in styles for the student of twentieth-century sculpture.

The centerpiece for the park is undeniably the *Unisphere* (6), the monumental steel globe that still dominates the entire area. Built for the 1964 World's Fair (a gift from U.S. Steel), the unisphere gives a see-through vision of the earth, its continents in place with giant latitude and longitude lines forming a grid of steel. While it may not precisely be deemed "art," it is nonetheless a striking construction. It is best viewed from a slight distance, though you will probably enjoy walking (or riding your bike) up to it, to experience its size and design more closely. Among the statistics you might consider are the following: the unisphere is 140 feet high, 120 feet in diameter, and it weighs 700,000 pounds.

Between the Queens Museum and the unisphere you'll find an empty pool that once decorated the World's Fair of 1964 and was ornamented by a picturesque fountain, *Armillary Sphere* (7), designed by the sculptor Paul Manship. Manship's fountain was made up of fanciful versions of the twelve signs of the zodiac, but over the years, some of the zodiac figures disappeared. Aries the Ram and Taurus the Bull, each 2 feet high, were just recently recovered and will perhaps be reinstated by the time you take this walk. The fountain was originally donated by the Fair to New York to honor the city's three hundredth birthday. (Unfortunately today it no longer functions as a fountain.)

The Queens Museum (8) is a lively and "au courant" place that houses a variety of interesting exhibitions and events. Among recent shows were "Television's Impact on Contemporary Art," "Classical Myth and Imagery in Contemporary Art," "New British Painting," "The Pattern and Decoration Movement," and an exhibition of Keith Haring works. In addition to these current themes, the museum has devoted exhibitions to "Remembering the Future: The 1964 World's Fair" and "Classical Sculpture from Ancient Greece." Dozens of events take place at the museum, from workshops to films, lectures to celebrations. If you wish to coordinate your Flushing Meadows outing with a particular exhibition, call (718) 592-5555 for information.

No matter what the current exhibition is at the museum, you can always see the *Panorama,* a must-see exhibition upstairs in the small building. (Children will particularly enjoy this construction, as will any and all New Yorkers or New York enthusiasts.) The world's largest architectural scale model, this extraordinary structure shows all five boroughs of the city in precise and fascinating detail. Built at a scale of 1 inch to 100 feet, it includes every important building in the city and is constantly updated. Originally constructed as the featured exhibit of the New York City Pavilion at the 1964 World's Fair, the *Panorama* was an immediate success; it still is a major tourist attraction and teaching tool for the city's children (various neighborhoods can be lighted and studied). Over 865,000 buildings are represented, as well as the city's rivers, hills, bridges, and trees. The total panorama covers more than 9,000 square feet. A flyer at the museum will give you many more precise and interesting details.

To the right, a short distance from the museum, you'll find the *Time Capsule* (9), where items from 1964 were saved. Another reminder of the 1964 World's Fair is the New York State Pavilion (10), now a big, empty circular space with an intriguing floor that will particularly entice children and residents of New York State. Almost all of an enormous mosaic map of the State of New York still covers the pavilion's floor. It is so detailed that you can probably spot your old hometown or the route you take to the Adirondacks in the still-bright mosaic bits that make up this very unusual floor. (There is also an echo here—a reminder of the dilapidated state of the old World's Fair buildings that remain.)

Our final stop is the *Marble Bench* (11) commemorating the site of the Vatican Pavilion in the 1964 World's Fair. A circular bench and a dais made of granite, the pavilion once exhibited Michelangelo's *Pietà*. But today it is merely a nice resting spot, which you might welcome after your long bike ride.

Nearby, the Queens Botanical Garden, at 43–50 Main Street and Dahlia Avenue, is a pleasant 38-acre park (once a dumping ground), of which about half is dedicated to formal plantings. You'll enjoy the Perkins Memorial Rose Collection (with its more than four thousand bushes), a rock garden, herb garden, and specialized garden for birds and bees. There is even a fragrance garden for the blind. In spring, flowering cherry trees, crabapples, and thousands of bright tulips add their magic, while in fall you can enjoy a wonderful display of colorful chrysanthemums. Queens Botanical Garden is a small but attractive spot to visit, with flat terrain for easy walking. The Garden also sponsors a variety of year-round workshops on such topics as Japanese-style dish gardens and hanging gardens for indoor or outdoor use. Telephone: (718) 886-3800.

INFORMATION

The park is open all the time, year round and is wheelchair accessible, as is the museum. No admission fee. Telephone:

(718) 699-6722. Queens Museum: open Tuesday–Friday, 10–5; Saturday and Sunday, noon–5:30. Closed Mondays.

DIRECTIONS

Subway: #7 train to either Willets Point-Shea Stadium station or 111th Street station.

Car: Take Queens-Midtown Tunnel and the Long Island Expressway (Route 495) or the Triborough Bridge and the Grand Central Parkway. Exit at Shea Stadium and follow signs into park. Parking on premises.

26

A New England Village Walk

Litchfield, Connecticut

This is a walk through a rare, unspoiled New England town. Litchfield is a village that has managed to retain its Colonial character for almost 300 years. The visitor arriving here is astonished by the seemingly endless rows of perfect eighteenth-century white houses, the elegant Congregational Church poised above the town green, the cobblestone courtyards of shops. But Litchfield is not a reconstruction or a self-conscious preservation effort; it has been able to retain its architectural integrity by vigilant citizen effort and through accidents of geography and history. Yet it is a bustling town with lots to see within a relatively concentrated area.

Litchfield has an illustrious history for such a small place: It was home to the nation's first law school and the first seminary for girls; the eighteenth-century home of Connecticut's chief justice is found here as well as the 1787 parsonage where Harriet Beecher Stowe's father lived. Litchfield was a small but well-to-do Colonial and Federalist settlement, as can be seen from the grandeur of its early homes.

In 1719 Litchfield was incorporated in the Connecticut Assembly, divided into 60 homesteads each of 15 acres. Some of these can still be visited. The colonists prospered, and soon Litchfield became an important stagecoach stop be-

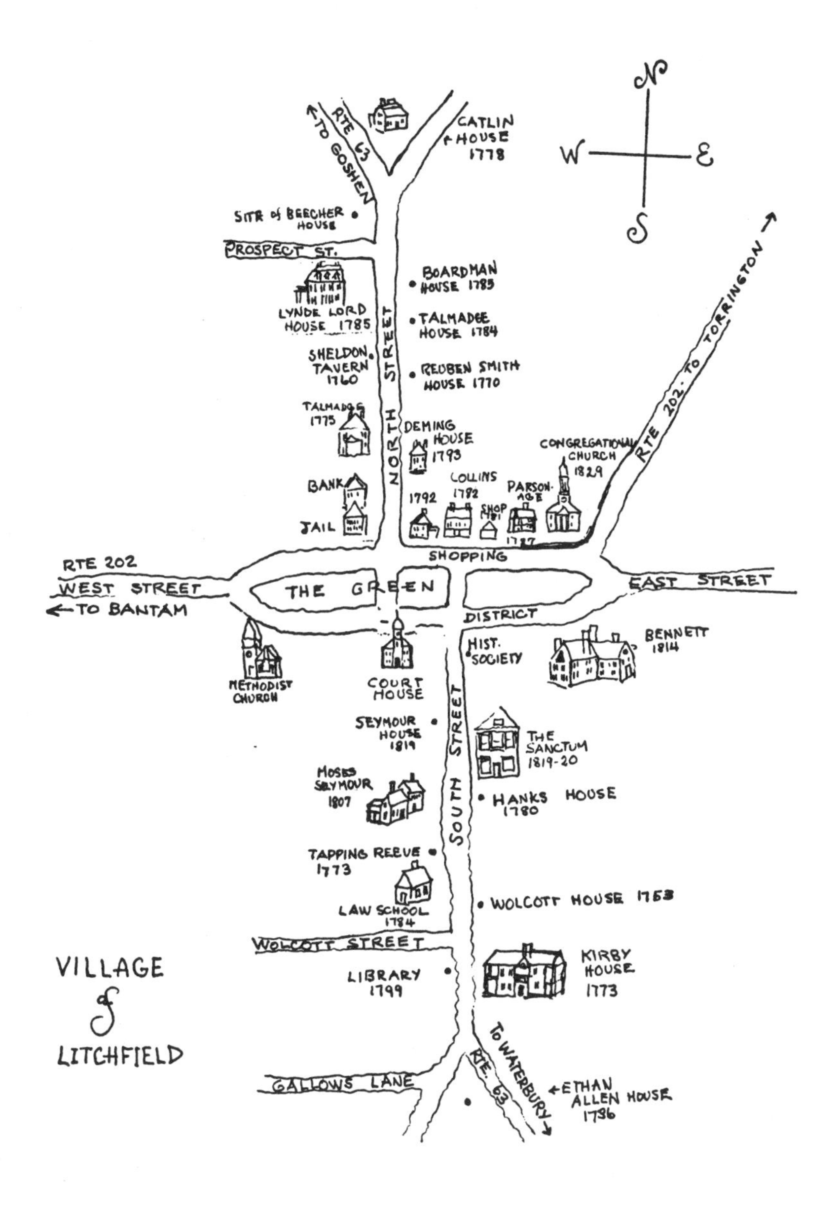

tween Boston and New York, and Albany and New Haven. In 1751 it was chosen to be county seat. By the time of the Revolution, Litchfield, strongly on the patriot side, provided as many as 500 men to the effort. Among the Revolutionary tales is one describing how an equestrian statue of George III was toppled in New York City and dragged all the way to Oliver Wolcott's woodshed on South Street in Litchfield, where it was melted down into bullets by the local ladies. And, we should add, both Lafayette and Washington slept here—many times.

Litchfield citizens became prominent in many fields. Tapping Reeve (not an original landowner) started the nation's first law school in 1774; among its students were Aaron Burr (Reeve's brother-in-law), three Supreme Court justices, 28 Senators, and more than 100 Congressmen. Here Sarah Pierce opened her Female Academy, the first school for young ladies' higher education in the country. By the 1850s, when railroads brought people and prosperity, Litchfield was left behind. In 1859 it was still the only four-horse stagecoach stop on the Naugatuck Road. As it escaped industrialization, it became a haven for retired people, summer visitors, and eventually for commuters attracted by the quiet charms of the village and surrounding hills. In 1913 the White Memorial Foundation incorporated to preserve the area including Bantam Lake; some 5,000 acres are devoted to a bird sanctuary, wild gardens, and recreational facilities. And in 1959 Litchfield itself was designated a historic area. Tapping Reeve's law school and the village green, as well as areas of both North and South streets, are registered National Historic Sites.

This outing will appeal to those with an interest in architecture, craft shops, and Americana, young and old alike. Pick up a walking tour map at the information center on the village green for a detailed guide to each house. A Colonial architecture guide is a good idea if you're interested in such details as eaves, roof lines, and fan windows. This walk is not difficult or long (covering about one square mile), and there are many places to stop for refreshment or rest.

Litchfield is nice at any time of the year. Because of its

location at the foot of the Berkshires, the fall foliage is particularly glorious. Nearby attractions at Bantam Lake make it a good summer excursion as well, although summer visitors may find it a bit crowded. There are two special annual events that might make you want to visit at a particular time:

The Fall Foliage Rally, held at White Memorial Foundation on a Sunday in early October, is an event children will especially enjoy. Horses and ponies pull carriages and wagons in a series of races. Children are welcome to ask for free rides between competitions. Call (203) 354-6507 for information.

The annual tour of selected historic houses occurs on the second Saturday of July (for a small fee). Call the chamber of commerce at (203) 482-6586.

A first glimpse will make you want to explore this picture-postcard New England village, the village green, the broad tree-lined avenues, and the charming side streets. The historic district lies right in the center of town along the green, and North and South streets, which are each about .5 mile long. As mentioned before, we suggest stopping by the information center on the village green to pick up a map. You will walk past stately Colonial homes, uniformly white with black shutters, that have been occupied by governors, justices, and senators through the years, as well as the birthplaces of Ethan Allen, Henry Ward Beecher, and Harriet Beecher Stowe.

Your walk should begin with the church at the green. Proceed along the green by the parsonage (1787), past three small shops from the 1780s, and then north along North Street. At the watering trough, cross the street and start back on the other side, passing five homes, the bank, and the jail. At the green are the Methodist Church and the Court House. Along South Street you will find the Tapping Reeve House (1773) and many other interesting sites:

First Congregational Church is a fine example of the double-octagon steeple design. Built in 1829, it was moved in the

1870s; after functioning as a meeting place and movie house, in 1929 it was returned to its proper site on the green. Open daily.

Litchfield Historical Society and Museum in the Noyes Memorial Building exhibits Revolutionary period paintings, including those of Ralph Earl, as well as some furniture and law books, in an uncluttered and inviting setting. Open April through December, Tuesday through Saturday, from 11:00 A.M. to 5:00 P.M. (203-567-5862).

Tapping Reeve House and Law School, South Street, graduated over 1,000 notable students who contributed greatly to American society, such as Horace Mann, Aaron Burr, and John C. Calhoun. Inside the museum, dedicated to Judge Reeve, you can see fine antique furniture that belonged to the Reeve family and sundry historic mementoes. The tiny schoolhouse next door has on display handwritten ledgers of students and original law books. You can visit from May to October, 11:00 A.M. to 5:00 P.M.

Wolcott Memorial Library, South Street, exhibits paintings, sculpture and photography. Although the main library is new, it is attached to a 1799 house built by Oliver Wolcott, Jr., son of one of the signers of the Declaration of Independence. Open year round, Tuesday through Saturday.

Cobble Court, around the corner from the Historical Museum, is a well-appointed group of small shops featuring local handcrafts, clothing, imported yarns, new and old books, and cookware.

Sheldon's Tavern, North Street is another spot where George Washington actually slept.

INFORMATION

Most of the sites listed are wheelchair accessible and the town itself is mostly flat.

DIRECTIONS

From the west side of Manhattan: Henry Hudson Parkway (West Side Highway) to Saw Mill River Parkway to Interstate 684 north Route 84 east to exit 17; north on Route 63 to Litchfield. From the east side of Manhattan: FDR Drive, Major Deegan Expressway to Saw Mill River Parkway. Follow same directions as above.

27

A Walk Through a Methodist Village on the Shore

Ocean Grove, New Jersey

The village of Ocean Grove is a one-of-a-kind shore community. When you think of taking a walk in most shore towns near New York City, you usually find busy, commercial places with little charm. Not so with Ocean Grove. Located on the New Jersey shore one hour's drive south of the city, it contrasts sharply with its neighbors. This is a picturesque town of delightful Victorian gingerbread houses, small hotels, and tiny shops lining pleasantly shaded streets. A fine, wide promenade runs along the oceanfront. Of note is a giant architectural wonder—the Great Auditorium—and dozens of little painted structures for camp meetings.

Ocean Grove's location is what appealed to its founders, a group of Methodist ministers and lay people who, in 1869, came from Philadelphia to conduct a revival meeting. They pitched their tents in this quiet ocean retreat, creating a religious seaside resort in which to pursue annual summer meetings in relative isolation. Facing the ocean and flanked on both sides by two small lakes (Wesley Lake and Fletcher Lake), they thought the area was "removed from the dissipations and follies of fashionable water places." By 1874 the

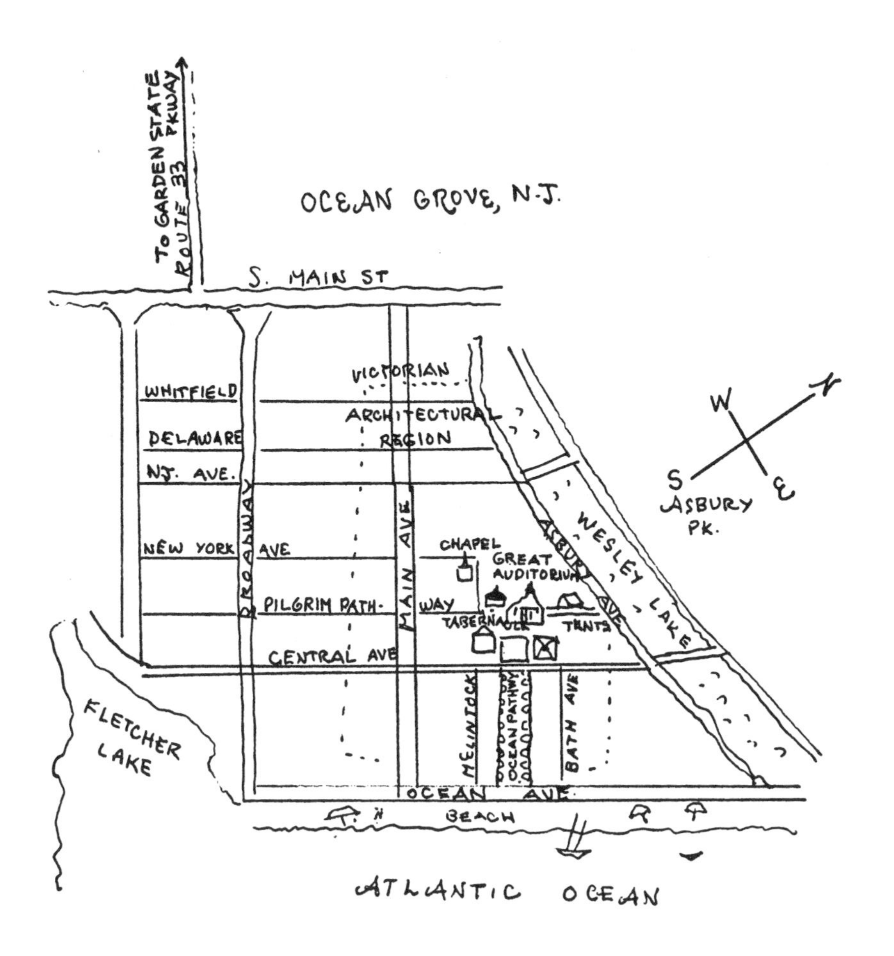

tent community—known as "little canvas village"—included about 200 ministers during the height of the season and almost 700 tents with permanent floors and small kitchens for the community. The Methodist Camp Meeting Association, which ran the community, remained a private association, so that it could maintain strict control over the inhabitants of the resort. Lots were leased for ninety-nine years, with the option to renew! Strict regulations included no alcohol, smoking, organ grinders, peddlers, vendors, or carriages on the beach; no swearing in boats on Lake Wesley, no newspapers on Sunday, no dancing, and no card playing. The gates of the resort closed daily at 10:00 P.M. and remained closed all day on Sunday. In fact, no one could do much of anything on Sunday—except attend religious meetings. Trains were not allowed to stop at the Ocean Grove/Asbury Park station (much to the annoyance of the inhabitants of Asbury Park), and no one could enter the community on Sunday except on foot (over the footbridges of Wesley Lake). Indeed, President Ulysses S. Grant, who once visited his mother and sister on a Sunday at their rented Ocean Grove Cottage, was obliged to walk into town, like anyone else. His carriage waited for him outside the town gates.

There *were* a few recreational outlets for visitors to Ocean Grove, however. They were allowed to stroll on the boardwalk and go boating on Wesley Lake. For some time the town fathers thought of banning swimming altogether (because of the inevitable disrobing it entailed), but they agreed to it, reluctantly, with some conditions. (Of course, swimming was forbidden on Sundays.)

Most of the life of Ocean Grove centered around the auditorium (which you can still visit), an immense and curious edifice built in 1894 to accommodate 10,000 people and a 500-person choir. (It was constructed without nails in imitation of Solomon's temple in the Bible.) Here, during camp meetings, religious services were held daily, on a continuous basis. Ocean Grove still holds religious and musical programs in this auditorium; indeed, the town remains a religious retreat for many, who still set up tents in summer. Although its blue laws have disappeared, it maintains a pristine and pure quality, which adds to its charm. (It was this special ambience that appealed to Woody Allen, when he chose it as the location for his film *Stardust Memories* some years ago.)

We think that walking through this unspoiled town, with its wonderful boardwalk and refreshing ocean breezes, makes for a pleasant outing for just about anyone, young or old. The atmosphere is relaxed and casual, conducive to a leisurely stroll. Unless people-watching is your favorite sport, we recommend a visit to Ocean Grove off-season, for even here there is inevitably more congestion and activity during the summer months. (And driving to and from the Jersey Shore in summer can be a nightmare.)

Park your car wherever you can, preferably along Main Avenue, in the center of town. We recommend you pick up a walking map, available at one of the realtors (or other shops) on the street. On Main Avenue you'll find many small shops and an array of Victorian houses with gingerbread porches, painted in the most original color combinations. Walk toward the ocean for your stroll along the uncluttered boardwalk. You'll see a fishing pier and two wide and well-maintained bathing beaches. After you have filled your lungs with the clean ocean air, you can begin your exploration of the rest of the town. Don't miss Ocean Pathway, a picture-postcard street lined with trees and park benches. You can understand why this street is often photographed: Rarely do you have the opportunity to see such a collection of charming and unusual Victorian houses. Make a detour or two to discover some of the other quaint streets that run parallel to Ocean Pathway, starting at Ocean Avenue. Of course the part of town that is of particular interest is the religious complex, including the Great Auditorium, the Tabernacle, the Founders Park, Thornley Chapel, and the remains of some of the tents. You can reach these surprisingly offbeat buildings by walking on Pilgrim Pathway, Central Avenue, or their cross streets. There are squares, pleasant parks, and curious little streets to see at every turn, and you can meander about as long as you like. Finally, you might enjoy walking across Wesley Lake (toward Asbury Park) on the same bridges that were used by many a Sunday walker 100 years ago. You'll notice a sharp contrast between the well-preserved Ocean Grove and its nearby urban neighbor.

After your walk you might enjoy a visit to Spring Lake, another pleasant waterfront village, about 15 minutes south of Ocean Grove.

INFORMATION

This oceanside village is flat and features a wheelchair accessible boardwalk.

DIRECTIONS

From midtown Manhattan take the New Jersey Turnpike south to exit 11 onto the Garden State Parkway south. Take exit 100B and Route 33 east. Follow signs to Ocean Grove.

From George Washington Bridge take Route 80 to the Garden State Parkway and follow same directions as above.

28

Hofstra University Arboretum: Gardens and Sculpture

Hempstead, New York

It may surprise you to discover that the campus of Hofstra University, which from the outside appears to be an ordinary contemporary college campus with tall, modern buildings, is in fact much more. Within its gates you'll find an extraordinary arboretum and outdoor sculpture collection. A walk on the grounds, along the pleasant, flat walkways, amid sculptures, courtyards, trees, shrubs, and colorful flower displays, is in every way a satisfying experience, combining art and nature.

This is an outing you can either do on your own, with a walking guide in hand, or with others as part of a tour. Although you are welcome to visit the campus at any time of the year, you might wish to come in spring or summer, when the gardens are at their best; or you might prefer a quieter time, when you can still enjoy the sculptures just the same.

The university was named after William Hofstra, a local businessman of Dutch origin, whose 15-acre estate was bequeathed to it for "scientific or research purpose" and became the nucleus for the college. Since its inception in the 1930s it has expanded to its present 238 acres, and has been considerably embellished with the addition of many wonderful plantings and artworks.

The idea for a sculpture park began in the late 1960s, when *Knight,* by Manolo Pascual, was first displayed on the grounds. Over the years the works of many well regarded artists, local and otherwise, have been added to the collection. Today the forty or so, mostly contemporary, sculptures represent one of the largest and most impressive art collections on Long Island. The works have been carefully placed within the grounds in such a way as to enhance them and their surroundings, and most are identified. You'll see the rounded forms of a Henry Moore amid groupings of conifers; an unmistakable Seward Johnson figure; a brushed steel abstraction by Antoni Milkowski on a grassy plot; and a Constantino Nivola sculpture, looking like a small, ancient monument discreetly set below a large Norway maple. The Hofstra Museum, as the exhibition space is called, also includes four indoor galleries and other locations around the campus where art works can be enjoyed.

Like the sculpture park, the arboretum is spread throughout the entire Hofstra campus. In fact, the university itself was designated as a "national arboretum" in 1985 by the American Association of Botanical Gardens. Included are some 7,000 trees representing well over 200 varieties, both native and exotic; among the rare specimens are a Himalayan pine, a bald cypress, a Chinese quince, and an umbrella pine. (Most of the trees are labeled.) You'll also find an abundance of annuals and perennials. Masses of bulbs—particularly the thousands of tulips that have been cultivated to celebrate Hofstra's Dutch heritage—transform the arboretum into a magical color fantasy in spring. An exquisite collection of shrubbery—witch hazel, forsythia, Korean azaleas, mock orange, rhododendrons, viburnums, and lilacs, among others—adds more brilliance and perfumes the air.

Before you begin your walk, you'll want to find a place to

leave your car (not always an easy task when school is in session). Try parking either in the area near the Student Center (on the north campus, on your right as you are heading west on the Hempstead Turnpike) or behind the Spiegel Theater (on your left). If you park at the Student Center you can cross the road via the "unispan" (rather uphill) to Hofstra Hall, in the center of the campus, where we suggest you begin your walk. You will want to pick up a walking guide for both the arboretum and the sculpture park, available either at Hofstra Hall or at the Hofstra Center (on the corner of Hofstra Boulevard and Hempstead Turnpike), where you can also arrange for a guided tour.

Hofstra Hall, the gracious country home of the Hofstra family, was at first the only campus building besides the bookstore and the few athletic facilities. Since those days it has been lovingly refurbished and is worth a visit.

Just in front of Hofstra Hall is a sculpture you won't want to miss, J. Seward Johnson Jr.'s *Creating.* This 1982 work portrays in Johnson's superrealistic style a seated man reading a book under a shady locust, much like any college student or professor might do on a lovely day.

Nearby, on a walkway on the edge of the Pinetum, you'll find the wonderful Henry Moore work, *Upright Motive No. 9,* perhaps the most important sculpture in the collection. Surrounded by a low, circular brick wall, it is an imposing vertical figure with strong, fluid lines. Moore created it in 1979 as part of a series in which he was exploring the placement of form.

While at this spot you can enjoy the remarkable collection of evergreens that form the Pinetum, among them the bald cypress, oriental spruce, weeping hemlock, Korean pine, Katsura tree, and weeping nootka fake cypress.

As you wander around the spacious grounds you will find many other sculptures of interest, including: Arthur Gibbons's *See,* a grouping of steel creations that seem to be organically connected to their surroundings; David Jacobs's *Crossing the Channel,* a welded aluminum contrapuntal abstraction; Tony Rosenthal's *Black and Blue with a Little Red,* a brilliant painted steel work of imposing proportions; Dolly Perutz's *Introvert and Extrovert* and *Pelican,* both inspired by Klee; Penny Kaplan's *Lost Splendor,* a collection of stark white columns reminiscent of ancient Greece; Robert White's *Con Grande,* an equestrian statue inspired by a Gothic monument in Verona, Italy; Ibram Lassaw's *Homage à Weller,* an intricate bronze abstraction; Phyllis Mark's *Land Sail II,* an aluminum work of constantly moving geometric patterns; and another J. Seward Johnson, Jr., *Hitchhiker,* with the subject hoping to get to Boston.

You can also discover a model bird sanctuary, a butterfly walk, a Shakespeare garden, and a sensory garden for the disabled.

While enjoying all or some of the above, you will probably come to the realization that there are more sculptures and plantings here than you can possibly take in at any one time. Happily, you are always welcome to return and enjoy Hofstra's many offerings.

INFORMATION

The Hofstra University campus is wheelchair accessible throughout and is open year-round. For information on tours, exhibits, or special events call the Admissions Office at (516) 463-6700.

DIRECTIONS

From New York City: Triboro Bridge to Grand Central Parkway, Eastern Long Island. Exit 31A, Meadowbrook Parkway south to Hempstead Turnpike (exit M4 West). Follow Hempstead Turnpike west to Hofstra, about 1½ miles.

29

Wave Hill: An Art/Nature Visit at an Elegant Hudson River Estate

Riverdale, New York

Wave Hill is one of New York City's less known gems. Although familiar to some, this rare botanical garden/art environmental center comes as a real surprise to most first-time visitors. Its picturesque setting high above the Hudson, with remarkable views on all sides, its formal gardens, vast rolling lawns dotted with huge old trees and environmental sculptures, and its acres of woodlands, make this 28-acre park a unique spot. And as you stroll by its two stately manor houses set in the plantings, you'll imagine you're enjoying a day at a private estate, miles away from the city.

In fact, in the past Wave Hill was the country home of several prominent New Yorkers. From the time the first of its two houses was built in 1848 by the jurist William Lewis Morris, it was occupied by illustrious people who often entertained members of New York society. As a boy, Teddy Roosevelt spent a summer here with his family, where it is said he learned to appreciate nature—birds in particular. William Makepeace Thackeray visited on occasion; Mark Twain lived here from 1901 to 1903 (and even built a treehouse on the grounds); and Arturo Toscanini occupied the house from

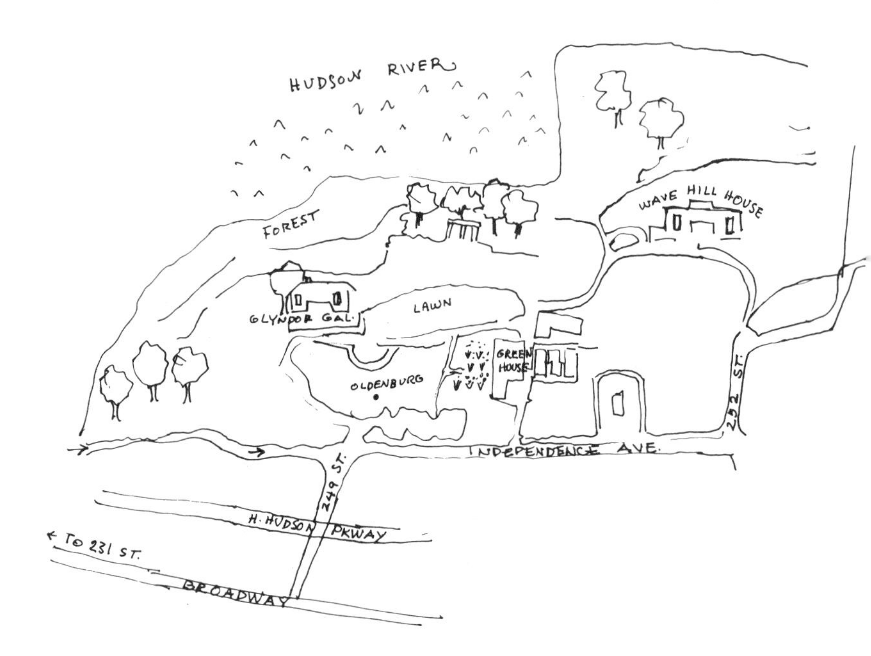

1942 to 1945. In the 1950s it was home to the head of the British delegation to the United Nations, and visitors included the Queen Mother, Anthony Eden, Harold MacMillan, and Konrad Adenauer. Most proprietors of Wave Hill were interested in preserving the incredible natural site from profiteering land developers and in further enhancing it with both formal and naturalistic landscaping. The financier George Perkins, who moved in during the 1890s, was particularly successful in securing Wave Hill's future. (A conservationist, he also led the movement to preserve the palisades and organized the Palisades Interstate Park.) He expanded the estate, adding greenhouses, gardens, orchards, pergolas, and terraces. Working with a landscape gardener from Vienna, he created an English landscape-style garden, mingling formal with informal plantings, and rare trees and shrubs with more common species. Many of these plantings still remain. In 1960 the Perkins family deeded the estate to New York City to become an environmental center for the enjoyment of everyone.

Today, Wave Hill (also called Wave Hill Center for Environmental Studies) is and does many things. It sponsors indoor and outdoor art shows (particularly outdoor sculpture shows throughout the vast grounds), horticultural exhibits, chamber music concerts, drama and arts festivals, and outdoor dance performances. There are ecological programs, lectures, craft workshops, and such special events as hawk watches and maple sugaring. And it is a place in which to enjoy both the thousands of remarkable plant specimens in the formal and wild gardens and the contemporary art scattered throughout the impressive grounds. A walk through this peaceful oasis will appeal to nature and art lovers alike, as well as to those who just want to get away from the chaos and noise of the city.

From the moment you walk through the gates, past the small parking area, and onto the meandering brick walkway, you know you're in a very special place—for the landscape has a feeling of space, with breathtaking views and grand vistas. At the same time it has intimacy and charm, unlike most institutional botanic gardens. The plantings have been designed on a small scale, so as to create a more personal environment, in keeping with Wave Hill's tradition as a private estate. And there is an atmosphere of peacefulness and ease. On nice days you might well see people sitting in the grass or in comfortable wooden armchairs scattered about in the lawn, enjoying the view, contemplating a work of art, reading, or just relaxing. Others may be sketching, photographing, or wandering among the various gardens.

Directly in front of the entrance is a nineteenth-century stone-columned pergola, a perfect lookout point to the Hudson and the palisades. To the right of the entrance is an enchanting flower garden, one of a collection of distinct plantings. This particularly luxuriant one combines old-fashioned varieties with less familiar plants, creating a carefree, romantic look. You will frequently see people examining the flowers with book in hand, admiring the colors and combinations, which are clearly the work of an artist (in fact, John Nally, who redesigned this garden, had worked as a print maker). Behind the flowers are the conservatory and greenhouses, with many exotic plants; an enclosed herb garden, with over one hundred varieties; a "wild" garden, with perennials and shrubs of different sizes and shapes arranged in a naturalistic way; an aquatic garden surrounded by shaded, trellised walkways; and more expanses of lawns and forests beyond.

As you wander from one garden to the next, you'll see contemporary outdoor sculptures in the grassy areas. Most of them are temporary exhibits that are shown for only a few months at a time, although two are on long-term loan: Claes Oldenburg's *Standing Mitt with Ball* (1973), a whimsical steel and lead baseball mitt holding a wooden ball; and Robert Irwin's *Wave Hill Wood,* remaining from his 1987 exhibition at Wave Hill. Irwin's group of ceremonial stone markers is set apart. The series of statuary begins at the roadside, continues across a grassy field, and ends in a wooded trail. The wanderer is invited to leave the road and experience both art and nature more intimately. In fact, the works shown at Wave Hill are commissioned and then installed in such a way as to harmonize with their surroundings; their materials and shapes blend with the natural landscape.

The works exhibited indoors are also of an environmental nature. They are shown in the two manor houses, Wave Hill House and Glyndor House. The older of these, Wave Hill House, is a handsome nineteenth-century fieldstone building with white shutters, ivied halls, and a vast terrace overlooking the river. Inside are several gallery rooms. One recent exhibit consisted of bold black and white wall drawings of plant life by Mike Glier. Next to the gallery space is Armor Hall, where chamber music is performed frequently. At Wave Hill House you can pick up a map of the area, as well as sundry pieces of literature and brochures relating to exhibits and subjects of horticultural interest. One series of pamphlets gives detailed information on conifers (among the most ancient plants on earth), with a self-guided tour among Wave Hill's varied and rich collection. (All the conifers on the grounds are labeled.)

Glyndor House, the other indoor gallery, is a red brick Georgian Revival–style house built in the 1920s. The exhibition space here is particularly appealing and bright; the airy white-walled rooms with their delicate moldings and gleaming wideboard wood floors provide an ideal setting. When we last visited we viewed a contemporary sculpture show of natural wood pieces by the abstract artist, Jene Highstein; his larger pieces were being exhibited outside in the lawns.

INFORMATION

Wave Hill is located at 675 West 253rd Street at Sycamore Avenue. We recommend visiting on weekdays (when Wave Hill is free and never crowded), although the estate is open seven days a week, all year, 9:30–4:30 except for Christmas and New Year's Day. In summer, the hours are extended. Note: Glyndor House Gallery is open Tuesday–Sunday, 10–4:30; Wave Hill House Gallery is open Tuesday–Saturday, 10–4:30. The greenhouses are open only from 10–noon and 2–4. Wave Hill is mostly wheelchair accessible. Telephone: (718) 549-3200.

DIRECTIONS

Subway: #1 train to 231st Street. Switch to BX 10 or 7 bus at northwest corner of 231st Street and Broadway. Walk across parkway bridge and turn left. Walk to 249th Street, turn right at Independence Avenue, and follow signs to Wave Hill gate.

Or A train to 207th Street; switch to BX 100 bus at 221st and Ishman streets (Broadway corner) to 252nd Street and walk to 249th Street, as above.
Car: Take the West Side Highway (Henry Hudson Parkway) up to Riverdale. After the Henry Hudson Bridge toll booths, take 246th Street exit. Drive on the parallel road north to 252nd Street, where you turn left and go over the highway. Take a left and drive south on the parallel road to 249th Street and turn right. Wave Hill is straight down the hill. Limited parking on the grounds and street parking.

30

Green Acres: An Animal Kingdom Made of Yew

Portsmouth, Rhode Island

If you like animal sculptures prettily set along garden paths—and wish to see some whimsical examples that are neither stone nor steel—make a visit to this topiary garden where growing trees and bushes are trimmed into myriad shapes, both abstract and realistic. Green Acres is a small estate whose gardens are filled with members of the animal kingdom, including a giraffe, a giant camel, a bear, a swan, an elephant, a rooster, and even a unicorn, all made of greenery. Set into a formal garden of flowers and hedges and geometric pathways, these cavorting animals are a particular delight to children.

Green Acres, not far from Newport, overlooks Narragansett Bay. It is the oldest topiary garden in the country. The seven-acre estate includes a summer house with original furnishings from its nineteenth century past and a toy collection, but it is particularly the topiary garden that draws visitors.

Green Acres garden was the idea of a family named Brayton who were enchanted by topiary gardens they had seen in the Azores. They and their gardeners, Joseph Carreiro (a native of the Azores) and his son-in-law, George Medonca, designed the gardens, beginning their work around 1893.

Green Acres' sculptures, made from nature, are both realistic and fanciful. The garden includes about one hundred pieces of topiary art, including geometric shapes, arches and ornamental designs, and some twenty-one animals and birds. The topiary works are made from yew and privet. Other specialties of the garden are thirty-five seasonally planted flower beds in the most perfect condition. There are peach trees and fig trees and grape arbors and various other horticultural pleasures.

In pleasant weather children can sit on tiny animal-shaped rocking chairs out among the topiary fantasies. Green Acres is included in a combination ticket with several of the mansions of Newport, or can be visited separately (at what we thought was an unfortunately rather steep price). If you would enjoy visiting Newport's great houses with their elegant period furnishings and art, however, the combination ticket is well worth the cost.

INFORMATION

Green Acres is on Cory's Lane in Portsmouth. It is open daily from 10:00 A.M. *to 5:00* P.M. *from May to November. There is a moderate admission charge. Wheelchair accessible. Telephone: (401) 847-6543.*

DIRECTIONS

From Providence take I-95 at the Wyoming exit and Route 138 east to Newport. At junction of R.I. 138 and Route 114, take 114 and continue for about seven miles north to Cory's Lane. Entrance is on the left.

Regional Index

Choosing an Outing

Gardens: Indoor and Out

Colonial Park, (NJ)	Chapter 1
Snug Harbor, (NY)	Chapter 2
Old Westbury, (NY)	Chapter 6
Aspet, (NH)	Chapter 8
Brooklyn Botanical Garden (NY)	Chapter 9
Longwood (PA)	Chapter 15
Wethersfield (NY)	Chapter 19
Smith College (MA)	Chapter 23
Hofstra University (NY)	Chapter 28
Wave Hill (NY)	Chapter 29
Green Acres (RI)	Chapter 30

Village Walks and Architectural Pleasures

Southport (CT)	Chapter 3
Usonia (NY)	Chapter 12
Litchfield (CT)	Chapter 26
Ocean Grove (NJ)	Chapter 27

Sculpture Parks and Outdoor Art

Snug Harbor (NY)	Chapter 2
De Cordova Museum (MA)	Chapter 4
Aspet (NH)	Chapter 8
PepsiCo (NY)	Chapter 11
Georgian Court College (NJ)	Chapter 13
Chesterwood (MA)	Chapter 18
Battery Park City (NY)	Chapter 20
Philadelphia Region (PA)	Chapter 21
Long Island City (NY)	Chapter 22
Flushing Meadows (NY)	Chapter 25
Wave Hill (NY)	Chapter 29

College Campus Outings

Princeton University (NJ)	Chapter 5
Georgian Court College (NJ)	Chapter 13
Smith College (MA)	Chapter 23
Hofstra University (NY)	Chapter 28

With Children in Tow

Snug Harbor (NY)	Chapter 2
De Cordova Museum (MA)	Chapter 4
Princeton University (NJ)	Chapter 5
The Cloisters (NY)	Chapter 7
Rockland Lake (NY)	Chapter 10
PepsiCo (NY)	Chapter 11
Nyack (NY)	Chapter 14
Battery Park City (NY)	Chapter 20
Long Island City (NY)	Chapter 22
Rockefeller State Park (NY)	Chapter 24
Flushing Meadows (NY)	Chapter 25
Green Acres (RI)	Chapter 30

Museums and Artist's Homes

De Cordova Museum (MA)	Chapter 4
The Cloisters (NY)	Chapter 7
Aspet (NH)	Chapter 8
Cole House and Olana (NY)	Chapter 16
Chesterwood (MA)	Chapter 18
Wethersfield (NY)	Chapter 19

Guided Tours Available

Princeton University (NJ)	Chapter 5
Old Westbury (NY)	Chapter 6
The Cloisters (NY)	Chapter 7
Brooklyn Botanical Garden (NY)	Chapter 9
Longwood (PA)	Chapter 15
Olana (NY)	Chapter 16
Chesterwood (MA)	Chapter 18
Wethersfield (NY)	Chapter 19
Noguchi Museum (NY)	Chapter 22
Smith College (MA)	Chapter 23
Hofstra University (NY)	Chapter 28
Green Acres (RI)	Chapter 30

Nature Walks

Rockland Lake (NY)	Chapter 10
Nyack (NY)	Chapter 14
Canal Towpath (PA and NJ)	Chapter 17
Rockefeller State Park (NY)	Chapter 24

Also by Marina Harrison and Lucy D. Rosenfeld:

ART ON SITE $16.95
Country Artwalks from Maine to Maryland

ARTWALKS IN NEW YORK *Second Edition* $14.95

A WALKER'S GUIDEBOOK $13.95
Serendipitous Outings Near New York City

To order, please send a check for the listed price to:
Michael Kesend Publishing, Ltd.
1025 Fifth Avenue
New York, NY 10028
Add $4.00 for shipping and handling plus 50¢ for each additional copy with the same order.
For quantity discounts, contact the special sales department at:
Tel: 212 249-5150
Fax: 212 249-2129